T0162067

A BOOK OF
COMMON PRAISE

Robert Boyers

AUSABLE PRESS
2002

Cover art: Tullio Pericoli, "Colpo d'Occhio" ("The Overview"), reproduced by permission of the artist.

Design and composition by Ausable Press. The type face is Adobe's Jenson. Cover design by Rebecca Soderholm.

Published by:
AUSABLE PRESS
46 East Hill Road, Keene NY 12942
www.ausablepress.com

LIBRARY OF CONGRESS CATATLOGING-IN-PUBLICATION DATA
Boyers, Robert.
    A book of common praise / Robert Boyers.
        p. cm.
    ISBN 1-931337-02-0 (alk. paper) – ISBN 1-931337-03-9 (pbk. : alk.
        paper)
        1. American literature–20th century–History and criticism. 2. English
        literature–20th century–History and criticism. I. Title.

PS221 .B57 2002
810.9'005–dc21
                                                    2002071652

A BOOK OF COMMON PRAISE

For Peg and our children,
and for Don McCormack.

FICTION WRITERS

Introduction to a Book of Introductions

Recently, hearing that I was to bring out a book of introductions—of all improbable things—one of my writer friends asked whether I didn't feel 'funny' publishing a book so full of praise. I am, after all, and have long been, a practicing literary critic, someone whose business is to discriminate, assess, recommend, resist. Have I not often had, my friend went on, knowing the answer but persisting nonetheless, rather harsh or at least less than favorable things to say about a new book? Did I not, in fact, sometimes relish the prospect of saying *no*, whereas in a book of introductions, I would necessarily be saying, in ever so many ways, *yes?*

Well, surely, yes, I have often done, and with pleasure, the work of the critic. And yes, the work of the introducer is a different sort of thing. To 'bring on' a speaker at a public event, after all, is principally to assume the role of appreciator, evoker, describer. More than occasionally, it is to speak as a lover. Where criticism is—or so I take it to be—disinterested, though full of conviction, introductions are an expression of one person's enthusiastic commitment to the work of a writer an audience has assembled to hear.

No doubt a good introduction at a public event will contain elements of criticism, including discrimination and assessment. Presumably the enthusiast will have engaged the work of an author more or less disinterestedly before agreeing to offer an introduction. But it is clear that resistance—genuine, protracted resistance—is out of place in an introduction, and if resistance is wanted or missed in the pieces that follow, I can assure my reader that resistance was the last thing wanted in the events for which my introductions were originally conceived.

I delivered my first few introductions in 1965, and since then I suppose I have presented a thousand or more. In the past fifteen years, as director of the New York State Summer Writers Institute at Skidmore College, I have delivered between twenty-five and thirty-five introductions each July, trying to find inventive ways to sustain the interest of diverse audiences already disposed to be enthusiastic, but also doing my best to surprise and stimulate the writers themselves, many of whom return year after year to our program and patiently listen to me introduce them, in some cases for the tenth or twelfth or fifteenth time. The situation is bound, no doubt about it, to produce in the poor writer a species of tedium, an unbearable sense of déjà vu, or, occasionally, the grateful sense that somehow something new under the sun can still be said about a writer whose gifts and propensities have long been common knowledge.

In 1977 I was asked to introduce, on a single evening, the poet Ben Belitt and the critic George Steiner on the occasion of the first annual Ben Belitt Lecture at Bennington College. Steiner was to deliver the opening lecture in a series that has by now lasted for twenty-five years. The introductions I delivered in the seventies tended to last not more than three or four minutes each, but President Joseph S. Murphy of Bennington College insisted that these inaugural introductions were to be elaborate affairs—"at least ten or twelve minutes apiece"—befitting an august occasion at which I would also bring on the elderly donor who had graciously endowed the lecture series in the name of her former teacher.

And so, for the first time, I dutifully composed, and delivered, one after the other, not one, but two rather elaborate, complex—some would say interminable—introductions, each in turn eliciting thunderous applause: first, a standing ovation for

Ben Belitt, and then an equally vigorous and lengthy ovation for George Steiner, who rose at last, gravely, from his seat on the platform, strode slowly, deliberately to the lectern, and leaned into the microphone to say, not plaintively but softly, "there seems to have been a misunderstanding. I thought I had been informed that I was to be the first Ben Belitt lecturer."

And so it has seemed to me, where introductions especially are concerned, that too much of a good thing—assuming that it is indeed a good thing—is, well, too much. I do not pretend to know precisely and in every instance what is too much or, indeed, too little, but I have hoped at least to make my introductions full enough to say something helpful and brief enough not to invite undue comparison with more expansive literary essays. What breathes in these introductions, I suppose, is the love of good writing and of honest writerly ambition, and they must in the end stand or fall on the communicated sense of that complex love.

—*Robert Boyers*

POETS

BEN BELITT [1990]

This is to be—so he tells me—Ben Belitt's final public reading. He is eighty years old, and he has done the thing often enough, he says, to feel no regret about giving it up. And so I say, in return, though I confess to the sly suspicion that we'll soon prevail upon him to renounce his decision, that I respect the wish to call an end to certain things, to assign to one's activities their proper time, place and measure.

This is not, by any means, to suggest that Ben is a poet of cautious measures and seemly proportions. He is, in fact, or much of the time, a poet of excess who typically prefers the more ornate and the lavishly colored to the smooth and plain. Though he aims for what he calls the "acidulous essence" and hopes, as he says, "to diminish excess," his characteristic manner is expansive, his diction extravagant, his music more than occasionally insistent, heavily accented. Howard Nemerov surely knew what he was talking about many years ago when he said of Ben that his long, arduous work as a translator had developed in him an instinct for the exact, "extortionate" word, but there is nothing bare or niggling about Ben's idiom. His tropes and variants multiply inexorably like orchards in bloom, the language buoyantly venturesome, ever testing the limits, rarely content to settle on a single formulation when several will do. No poet since the early Wallace Stevens has managed to make of impeccably well-made poems anything quite so audacious, theatrical, abundant, elusive.

Another term often used to describe Ben's poetry is "difficult"—difficult as in: fond of recondite allusions, unfamiliar words, odd, vagrant associations. To be sure, Ben is no kind of naked poet, and he did, after all, come of age in the era of high modernism when the obscurity of the poet was not thought to be a fatal affliction or occasion for alarm. And yet Ben's work is not obscure or remote, not willfully literary. What sometimes stuns or confounds is not the propensity for recondite allusion or the vagrant unfamiliar word so much as the coruscating volatility of Ben's idiom, his gift for surprising juxtapositions, for the virtuoso's flash and filigree, for combining gross materiality and spiritual aspiration. Ben's lines are alternately dry and exotic, sensual and austere. As one faithful reader has said, in Ben "the mitigations of *perhaps* attend even his most glorious confidences." The improbable and the mundane things of this world wrestle with one another as if there were some prospect of balance or surcease that might thereby be achieved.

But what emerges throughout the "semiotic pageant" of Ben's work is the specter of irreconcilability, both intractable and permanent. The poet's gift for metamorphosis and prestidigitation takes our reader's breath away and leaves the world mutable and incomprehensible, as it was surely meant to be. "If nothing is ever reborn," the poet intones in "Possessions," and thereby confronts the ever-beckoning, ever volatile "midrash of hieroglyphics" with which he tempts and enthralls us. Difficulty in this poet is neither willful nor mechanical. It is central to his way of seeing the world, a manifest of his affinity for the "stubborn heterogeneity" he admires in the Spanish poet Antonio Machado, among others.

Early in my epistolary acquaintance with Ben he wrote to me that "It is hard to be a posthumous poet." I knew what he meant, of course, knew that his work had not found the broad appreciative audience attracted by other American poets, so that he went on, as a writer, believing that, at best, he was providing for another age, some hypothetical "other" readership. In "This

Scribe, My Hand" he identifies, with no trace of self-glorification or undue hyperbole, with the strangled, diminutive Keats, addressing him hopefully, as he says, "in the posthumous way,/ on the flat of a headstone/ with a quarrier's ink, like yourself:/ an anthologist's date and an asterisk,/ a parenthetical mark in the gas/ of the pyramid-builders," making, in the end, a futile, brotherly gesture, a singular, delicate "surgeon's incision/ for solitude."

But to read the poetry of Ben Belitt is to be reminded, again and again, of an expansive fraternity, of the poets whose works echo in his, of the writers he has enlarged and made his own in his essays and translations and original revisionings of the tradition. Ben's work is, for many, many of us, alive and inspiriting, bearing with it the voices and spirits of his literary companions, about whose company he betrays no anxiety or misgiving. Here, we note, fresh and abundant, are the "delphic" incantation and "irrational" extravagance of Pablo Neruda, the "curious circuitions" and unabashed romantic ironies of Saul Bellow, the anguished, imponderable, "indispensable enlargements" of T.S. Eliot, the "dangerous game of the mot juste" celebrated by Marianne Moore and Elizabeth Bishop, the visionary infatuations of Hart Crane. All these and more are part of him and of all he knows.

No doubt, since I have the secret of making him feel extant, as Ben once wrote me, I might have done better here to tell amusing stories about him on an occasion like this. His friends surely know there are amusing stories to tell. But I have a fatal inclination to high serious solemnity, and Ben deserves a better story-teller. And so, without further solemnity or ado, I present to you Ben Belitt.

FRANK BIDART [1997]

In a characteristically probing critical examination of Frank Bidart, Louise Glück notes that change, for this poet, "is specious," and that his poems "do not triumph over damage and shame, they find no cure, no respite, but in the manner of the great tragedies, Bidart's voices protest." They protest, or so we infer, not generally against this thing or that, but against something larger, more pervasive than a particular turn or development in someone's life. The protest is an acknowledgment that our lives are not what we want them to be, not a complaint intended to provoke remediation. There is, as Louise notes, a sense in Frank's work of "the smaller bondage of individual life contained within the larger bondage of the species," and the protest is issued, variously, in different voices, of "the child, the done-unto, the passive watcher," the haunted, the bereaved. Where other poets want to settle scores and announce grievances, Frank betrays at every turn the "will toward responsibility" and "the guilt of detachment." He is implicated in the condition he protests. He accepts, he wishes not to accept, that the movement out of our common condition is illusion, so that the pattern of our lives may well be caught in the few lines from the magnificent long poem Frank recently completed, as in: "Four steps forward then/ one back, then three/ back, then four forward:/ . . . the illusion of movement without/ movement."

The mystical element in Frank's poetry has often been cited, but it is an elusive quality to define or to account for. It is not, in Frank's work, associated with a salvational scheme or with any of the milder consolations. If anything, the mystical element in Frank is to be associated with suffering, not with a belief in absolutes or in the remission of sin. Though nothing is conclusively transcended in Frank's poems, the prospect of transcendence is kept alive, if only as a reminder that the life we are living is not what we can decently want. The language of guilt and sin is present to remind us that the ordinary is invested with meaning, and that we are, or ought to be, watchful, alert to every "occasion of renunciation," as an early poem put it. But alert and watchful as one may be, we *feel* in this work a fatedness, so that we are bound to pass through, or endure, or perish by, what we are slated for. Of course there is struggle in the embrace of this fatedness. There is the sharp sense that we dread and willfully court dreadful things, more than half want even the "bewilderment, unease" and "distrust" we feel. The will to escape, to transcend, to experience freedom, is always matched by the inescapable sensation that the really crucial things are "unpossessable," rooted, dark.

To listen to Frank read from his poems is to be confirmed in our sense that he is a thoroughly eccentric poet. Using italics, capital letters, parentheses, and exclamation marks to direct our reading, he confers upon his work a nervous, restless energy which accords perfectly with the questing, obsessive character of his thought. That thought is focused on a wide range of subjects, from a schizophrenic young woman to the dancer-choreographer Nijinsky and the dark nights of the poet's own soul. But throughout the poems, including his most recent work, one feels a steady absorption in the question of love, its capacity to thwart or to assist one's development as a human being. No poetry of our moment is more revealing in its way of intimating what is often buried too deep for expression.

FRANK BIDART [1999]

For some time now—surely since the publication of his collected poems, *In The Western Night*, almost a decade ago—it has been clear that Frank Bidart is a major American poet. To acknowledge this is to assert that the range of his work is considerable, that he has introduced into our poetry a unique and unmistakable voice, and that understanding of any one of his poems is immeasurably enhanced by familiarity with all the others. Some would add to these assertions the fact that Frank is always in pursuit of big game, that his aim is nothing less than the exploration of what Louise Glück names the "conditions, the givens of human life, if human life is thought through and not merely lived through."

Of course it is not so immediately obvious that Frank is invariably in pursuit of the givens of human life. The words—givens of human life—suggest universal problems, familiar, immitigable circumstances, aspects of desire typically confronted by most of us all the time. And of course one's first encounter with a Bidart poem is likely to produce an impression not of universal desire or familiar circumstance but of immoderate emotions, exacerbated states of consciousness, situations rather more extreme and challenging than we are likely to associate with our own lives.

More, the accent of these poems is likely from the first to seem terribly anguished, so that we are not at all surprised, merely moved—merely—when we come upon the lines "I hate and—love. The sleepless body hammering a nail nails itself, hanging crucified." In another poet such lines might seem worked up or a rare moment of deep, twisted feeling. But Frank is so true to this emotional register, to this accent of anguish and torturous self-interrogation, that we accept it in him, accept it altogether—as Frank's true voice of feeling. Though we may struggle for a while against the implication in the work that such a voice can also be a true expression of our balked and contrary emotions, we come around to this necessary acceptance the more accustomed we become to the defenseless intensity of Frank's poetry.

Perhaps the oddest feature of Frank's work is the theatrical element. We accept entirely descriptions of the work which emphasize its affinity for the extremities of Greek or Shakespearean tragedy. In Frank, the theatrical is sometimes a matter of unusual circumstance—say, an unrelievedly harrowing life—, sometimes a matter of extravagant heightening devices built into the lines: italicized expressions, capital letters, exclamation marks.

As readers we come rapidly to regard these elements as constitutive features of Frank's universe and way of expressing emotion, just as we readily accept the rightness of the sometimes very long sentences, the movement within the line from descriptive to imperative, from flat objectively noted narrative to excruciating internal probing, the alternation from heightened utterance to an idiom verging on pure prose.

But whatever the seeming incompatibilities, there is always, up front or barely, briefly set to the side, the theatrical, the far reaches of excess and obsession. What saves the poems from morbidity, from too much excess, is the obvious desire of the poet to know, to uncover what is hidden, to feel what is genuinely cause for anguish, to test everything on his own pulses, never to stand back and disinterestedly collect interesting symptoms. Frank is, in his poems, an infatuate of the emotional life, at least half the time in love with dark things. He acknowledges, now and then, the civilizing virtues of detachment, reason, balance, but he is drawn inexorably to what Auden once called "the nervous and the nights," the "weeping anarchic" forces we can never put fully behind us. There is no cure for the condition, our condition, that Frank anatomizes, but there is no trace in his work of bitterness or of triumphal self-satisfaction in his ability to name our tumultuous fate. To read Frank is to feel oneself fully implicated in our common condition, secure only in the sense that definitive escape or removal is illusion. Dazed, yet grateful readers, we follow Frank, down to the place where the injured make what they can of their lives.

FRANK BIDART [2001]

In a poem by Frank Bidart called "The Yoke," the speaker addresses, or invokes, his lover in words that include, "see upon my shoulders is the yoke/ that is not a yoke." The words are at once the expression of a lover's submissive resignation to his own enthrallment and, more obscurely, the statement of an entire disposition to which we dare not assign a single reductive epithet. The word 'see' at the front of the line, "see upon my shoulders is the yoke/ that is not a yoke," nicely reminds us that Frank's poems, many of them a species of dramatic monologue, are often clamorous in demanding our attention, seem often to grab hold of us and demand that we look at what we might well wish not to see. That the poems often vividly enact extreme states of feeling, rehearse, over and again, painful experiences, the making of fateful, irrevocable choices, is obvious. This is a poet given to the evocation of what he calls "baffled infatuations," "love and guilt," "fury and sweetness," and if his poems seem often to be dedicated to the proposition that "what you love is your fate," the poems are anything but programmatic. The disposition governing the work is restless and searching, alert to the presence of what Frank has called "the drained Spectres" and the voice, or voices, in his head. The yoke that is not a yoke is for this poet the fate that is feared and desired, loved not because it is good but because it may not be avoided or denied, and will therefore conduct us, in due course, to everything that is authentically ours.

This must not suggest that Frank is, in any conventional sense, a confessional poet who wears his own naked heart on his exposed and fluttering sleeve. Usually Frank speaks in voices not his own, adopts personae, masks, that allow him a theatrical, fully dramatic way into his subject. Though he offers, as he rightly calls it, "a poetics of embodiment," he is a poet deeply invested in form, and in forms. Readers swept off their feet by the raw urgency and power of Frank's poems, who therefore regard him as a poet given to blunt, unmediated utterance have simply chosen not to notice the elaborate narrative apparatus, the highly inflected rhetorical artifice, the carefully regulated pacing and variation that have marked Frank's work from its beginnings more than thirty years ago.

Frank's achievement as a highly original, idiosyncratic American poet is evident, unmistakable in his short poems as much as in the trademark longer poems. Even what look like slight works are typically intricate in their composition, made things employing the widest imaginable range of devices. A recent poem, less than half a page, called "Heart Beat," reinvents a re-iterated heartbeat that runs *less life less life*," and again, with increased power, *less life less life*," the music of the little poem insidious, so that one feels at once undone, though the ear retains the pleasure of the poem's dangerous, exhilarating movement from density and compression to a more deliberately elevated, somewhat anachronistic elegance. Hear, ever so briefly, the compression in the line—there's a bit of Gerard Manley Hopkins' music in it—"*creatures/ bred now for slaughter will/ Then never be bred.*" Then, please, listen to, "*still the vow solemn and implacable I made as a kid.*" The first of the quoted lines is deliberately difficult, feels deliberately cramped, pressurized. But the second line, "*still the vow solemn and implacable I made as a kid,*" has no trace in it of that other rhetoric, and is pleasing by virtue of its smooth numbers, its carefully adjusted syntax, its willing embrace of a diction—"*the vow solemn and implacable*"—that, in the hands of a less expansive poet, would seem not merely anachronistic, but formal, distant.

But of course artifice in Frank's work is never artificial, and the use he makes of the strategems he devises is such as to yield a consistenly communicated pressure of intensity and struggle. But let me end by saying, very plainly, that a poet like Frank, who has given us several of the best long poems ever written by an American poet, has no right—really—to surpass himself again and again. But at a stage when most other poets repeat themselves, Frank has been writing the very best poems he has ever written, and if I didn't think my time was more than up, I'd recite one or two short works and prove it.

LUCIE BROCK-BROIDO [1999]

"Toxic in a long day of fumes," the speaker says of herself
in a poem by Lucie Brock-Broido. Elsewhere she is "the red she/
Fox in habitat," or yet again, in another poem, "alive and vivid,
blessed by a season of high fever," "bold/ As a tendon arched in
the lover's hip." Are these, any of them, we wonder, declarations of
identity, lyric fragments together accumulating a reliable profile of
a person or a disposition? Such questions have only a little to do
with what matters most in the poetry of Lucie Brock-Broido, for
whom the action of a poem has principally to do with the rare intensities, the sudden swerves of diction and reference, the strange
varieties of music, that make her work thrilling and—with rare
exception—notoriously, wonderfully resistant to paraphrase.

One shrewd admirer of Lucie cites her "baroque voice," by
which, presumably, he means to identify a poetry of rare tensions,
mixed emotions and off-center oddities in diction, syntax, and
imagery. This is accurate, as far as it goes, and properly points us
toward the element of risk in a poetry that has little in common
with the safe, correct, tidy lyrics much preferred at many schools
of creative writing. Of course Lucie's poetry is impeccably well-
made, and early reviewers spoke routinely, as if it were obvious, of
the beauty of her poems, their perfection, their "brilliant timing,"
and other such qualities. But there is nothing of the merely well-
made in Lucie's poems, and one notes instead their drive, their
ferocity, their insatiability, their fanatic rage to get at the beautiful
and the life-giving. With these virtues, Lucie has opened up new
possibilities for American poetry, while reminding us of her connection—ambivalent, sometimes solicitous, sometimes preda-

tory—to predecessor poets like Emily Dickinson, John Berryman, even Sylvia Plath.

What one reviewer called the "neon" element in Lucie's first book, *A Hunger*, published in 1988, seemed at first to be an expression of her subject matter, which is sometimes the stuff of nightmare. One poem moves from the Nazi doctor Josef Mengele through a fire at an English soccer match and on to other comparable incendiary particulars. In another poem the ostensive speaker is Baby Jessica, the infant who captured national attention when she was trapped in a well-shaft. But as any reader of poetry knows, the description of subject matter in a good poem usually tells us very little about it. To come anywhere near Lucie's work is to note that it is not only disturbing but witty, that it is often most effective when it shifts into a mystical idiom, that it complicates its approach to contemporaneous or tabloid-tainted material by putting in our way arch mannerism, multiple voices, and a variety of formal devices. The power of Lucie's poetry has been from the first an achievement of style, of precision in the use of language, of control in the handling of tone and point of view. It is a reflection of Lucie's managed alternation between the focused and the out of focus, between neon and laser-beam, the fierce and the playful.

Lucie's second book, *The Master Letters*, has seemed to me and to others a magnificent and puzzling and irresistible work. Built around, or echoing, or taking off from three mysterious letters written by Emily Dickinson and discovered after her death, the fifty-two pieces collected in Lucie's volume range from inspired aphorism to highly charged prose, from the arcane to pastiche. In large measure an address to a masculine muse, part demon, part comforter, at best an ambiguous "master," the poems

15

in Lucie's book only occasionally summon the literal, substantial shape of Dickinson, and are least tied to her when they adopt a raucous idiom, when they see storms "like holy bowling balls down a long beige lane," or ask, in mock exasperation, "then why not buy a goddamn big Winnebago—and Drive," cast up Canadian dimes, "vending machines and roadside phones," the shades of "Louis Armstrong when he woke/ moonlit in his darkened room."

But however intermittent the swerves into contemporaneous dialect or reference, Lucie's poetry has about it throughout a wild music, an aura of possession and extravagance. Here, it declares, is no pallid little miss, "nobody's panther, ...no/ Midsummer naif in Havana rain," but one who can be "glad to see the summer dying/off." Dickinson's is but one occasional accent in a poetry of multiple registers, which can accommodate every kind of linguistic gesture, from the robustly plaintive—"I was cowering at the circumference/ of your heart"—to the erotic—"I will need the scarf about my mouth to Quiet me. I am overheated by hard riding,"—from the lugubrious and inspired—"light scars like the foxed pages of an old Germanic text; you mottle at the touch"—to the severe and aphoristic—"the difference between desire and compulsion/ is that one is wanting, one is warding off." And there is more, an unceasing shifting about that encompasses the flirtatious, the proud, the violent, the child-like and a dozen other accents. The wonder of it is that the voice should nonetheless seem singular—in all its diversity—and that it is never less than ravishing.

LUCIE BROCK-BROIDO [2000]

A week ago Lucie Brock-Broido delivered into my greedy hands the manuscript of eight recent, unpublished poems, and I thought I'd talk here not about, but around, those new works. They are, in every phrase and accent, Lucie, Lucie, Lucie, which is to say, fine-spun, flighty, eccentric, intricate, often oblique, but strangely, powerfully affecting. You listen to these poems, or read and re-read them, and you find yourself alternately pleasured and troubled, or troubled and pleasured all at once, so quick are the turns and reversals in the language, so unstable are the moods, even within poems that seem to grow out of a nameable sentiment or experience of loss.

You read in Lucie, let us say, of nightmares, and you note in the vicinity of the word *nightmares* itself familiar words like *regret* and *terrible* and *dread*. Yes, you say, this is what you are supposed to get in the realm of nightmare. But you also know that you are reading within a poem for which *nightmare* is apt to mean more, or other, a poem where contradiction is an intrinsic feature of everything said, where loss seems inextricably associated with victory, where defeat is registered as an inconsolable satisfaction. This is a realm in which you move without any hope of perfect clarity, though you have not the slightest doubt that every word has been chosen with perfect, perfecting scruple. The best you can do is to savor the coloring tensions and resist the temptation to resolve what resists resolution.

This is no easy effort we are asked to make, here or in others of Lucie's poems. It is not just that we like resolutions, that we are not often good with quandary or what Lucie calls "infinity of qualm." The problem is that we sense how much more than mere conundrum or abstract quandary is invested in the shifting terms of Lucie's poems. The problem is that we are with her, or think we ought to be, when she proposes to tackle something, to do this rather than that, to be strong rather than weak. We are with her and not certain where that is. When she tells us that "the nightmares have come back like women three/ times winding their hair in sullen braids," we are reluctant to decide how much or little to invest in that image of the women, though it haunts us more than a little. All we know is to follow on from one gorgeously mounted, quicksilver particular to the next, to listen patiently, as we go, for the next swerve, into wit or fierce laser-beam aphorism. The consolation of this progress we can almost name when we say that Lucie's poems put us in touch with what she calls, following Wallace Stevens, "an Ever."

So, what is an Ever? Lucie says it is, or was, "like a Jerusalem somewhere between fancy and imagination." She says it is, or was, "mostly poignant" and "cruel." And she says it is the condition of someone "wishing, specific, marooned," someone who knows what is "all deep, all deepening." Is this clear? If not, well, Lucie says that "if you don't fathom" her point, the Ever, "then you should not be reading"—or listening to—her poem, which may be fair enough, though you'd hate to think that an Ever could conceivably come between a reader and the pleasures to be derived from watching Lucie going through her turns and counter-turns, creating the images that seem to grow by natural and un-natural affinities, building and polishing and refining and lightly feeling her way, like an embodied, embodying spirit impatient for—Lucie's impeccable word—"the eventual."

LUCIE BROCK-BROIDO [2001]

I turn fervently to one of the new poems that Lucie Brock-Broido has lately given us, several of them published recently in *American Poetry Review*, and I read of an evening that "came like a millennium—that rare." Elsewhere, in another new poem, I read that "it is time, now, to sit still/ And run your finger along the suprasternum of/ The truth as it arches above the viscera." Is there, I ask, another poet in this country writing in anything remotely like that accent? Rare is one perfectly accurate word for a poetry that is not merely singular but elevated, its manner lavish, confident, its outlines pure and elegant as if it had been gone over by what Lucie calls a "rinsing wind."

That metaphor, Lucie's metaphor, of the "rinsing wind," may of course suggest several different possibilities, each of them carefully intimated in words, images which deftly guide our reading by putting in our minds the terms we need to navigate the uncertain waters of Lucie's poetry. In the poem called "Pyrrhic Victory," for example, we find the following terms: "slashing and burning," "tailored," "lavishly," "finespun," "refined," "absorbing everything," "liquid," "whisking." Not all of these terms are used in the same way, that is to say, with equal avidity or disdain or misgiving. But they do, all of them, set up a field of concerns, preoccupations, which the poet obviously wishes us to regard, directing us in the ways she takes to be appropriate for readers of her poetry.

Just so, we feel, do the words serve as reflexive markers directing the poet herself to consider what her own poems are doing, how they operate, and with what means and effects. Take Lucie's word "tailored," for example, as in "tailored/ Fields of gold."

That very expression has built into it a remarkable tension, for we cannot but be surprised by the use of a word like "tailored" in connection with "Fields of gold," which seems to us more lavish, more dream-like and rich than "tailored" can ordinarily be made to suggest. The point is that Lucie surely knows all that, and deliberately sets up, in the language she uses, in the contrasting yet somehow compatible textures and idioms of her poetry, a field of tensions that displays her own internal contradictions, her state of being-in-several-minds about what she wishes to accomplish as a poet and what, ultimately, is the true, indelible accent of her work.

Is she, in fact, as the language suggests, a tailored or tailoring poet, or is she lavish? Is she to be content with the rare, the dire, or is the price to be paid, in poetic terms, too great when a poetry is persistently rare, that is, a poetry so very beautiful, so clearly refined, so insistently elegant and perfect that it inspires in the poet herself what she calls—in the same poem—an "infinity of qualms"? Lucie's courage in naming the qualms, in calling our attention to them, is of course part of the pleasure we take in giving ourselves over to her, and though we permit ourselves also to be a little troubled by the intimated disturbances in Lucie's sense of what she is doing, we would have it no other way.

In fact, as we soon understand in reading Lucie's poems, contradiction is an intrinsic feature of everything said. This is a poet for whom loss is inextricably associated with victory, and defeat is registered as an inconsolable satisfaction. Lucie's poems describe, create a realm in which we move without any hope of perfect clarity, though we have not the slightest doubt that every word has been chosen with a perfecting scruple. If the truth in Lucie's poems "arches above the viscera" of ordinary reality, if the "Ever" in her poems is at once her goal and that which she can never quite bring herself to define, that condition of Lucie's imagination never seems to us less than fortunate. It is the ground, after all, of a poetry that can be gaudy and brittle, fervent and cool, poignant and cruel—cruel as in ferociously exacting, as in offering no easy victories, no resolutions. Lucie is at once intrepid voyager, perpetually "tomorrowing," as she likes to say, and intricate lace-maker, "quickened" and quickening in a "finespun" universe of her own delicate, exigent making.

JOSEPH BRODSKY [1995]

It is a very great pleasure to have with us today Joseph Brodsky, who has been regarded by other leading poets of our day—from the late W.H. Auden to Czeslaw Milosz—as one of the great poets of our time, and who won the Nobel Prize for literature in 1987. Indeed, he was singled out as the most gifted lyric poet of his generation by Anna Akhmatova when he was in his early twenties and had yet to offend the Soviet authorities. But offend them he did, by February 1964, when at twenty-four he was brought to trial on charges of social parasitism—a charming expression—and sentenced to hard labor for a period of five years, though he served only twenty months of that sentence. This did not prevent Mr. Brodsky from writing, and growing, and it did not prevent the Soviet authorities from inviting him to leave the country in 1972. To this courteous invitation we owe the good fortune of having had Mr. Brodsky among us in this country for the last twenty-two years. Among the enormous benefits of this arrangement I would count as singularly important Mr. Brodsky's evolving mastery of English, which has allowed him to write major essays in our language and to translate many of his own poems into an idiomatically rich and precise English that tempts us to think of him as one of our American poets. This idea may not please Mr. Brodsky, but it pleases those of us who have spent memorable hours with his poems—in English—as our companion.

It has often been remarked that Mr. Brodsky's muse is, in the main, a private, not a public muse, and that one should not be misled by his early troubles with the Soviet authorities to suppose that the key to his imagination is politics or rebellion. Fair enough, though one may be forgiven for reading—say, in a poem on the bust of Tiberius—references to monsters and "hell-bound fiends" as tokens of an imagination fully conversant with the vicissitudes of history, ancient and modern.

Auden was surely right to say, in an introduction to an early volume of Mr. Brodsky's poems, that they are rarely inclined to fortissimo, but one wants also to say that the range of Mr. Brodsky's effects is very broad, that his poems move from the dramatic to the grotesque, from the sombre to the comic, from the meditative to the ethereal. One feels in these alternations a deep responsiveness to a variety of traditions—the traditions of Russia and the traditions of poetry, of the church fathers and the literary mothers. One feels, as well, the sense of loss and uncertainty that figures in the poet's appropriations of tradition. This sense clearly reflects his deep understanding of our century as a time when entire civilizations may be threatened with deliberate extermination and traditions of every kind are routinely shuffled off with nothing like regret or reluctance.

Mr. Brodsky's meditations on the facts of life are properly alert to the prospect of sin and betrayal, and are at once chillingly ironic and mournful. Writing often with an intensity—and with a density of metaphor—that led Czeslaw Milosz to speak of him as a religious writer with an affinity for English metaphysical poetry, he seems nevertheless very much a poet of his time, often witty, playful, outré. To read him is to be reminded, again and again, of the pleasures and anxieties of exile, of language itself under threat of emptied meaning, of the struggle to confront love and death with measured seriousness. But what is most bracing in Joseph Brodsky's work is the range of resources mobilized even for the slightest of poetic tasks, our sense that through him we are in touch with countless voices and devices and sensibilities who have found in him extension and new life. He is a poet who expresses our moment and honors, perpetually, those who have come before him.

CARL DENNIS [1998]

Carl Dennis is a poet like no other. Of that I am certain —or as certain as a person who reads a lot of poems and knows a lot of poets can be. This is an odd and wonderful fact to think about. For Carl is not a showy poet. He doesn't aim to lead a movement or to discover a new poetic idiom. He writes, usually, about everyday objects and situations. Typically, he sets his tiny dramas in places utterly familiar. Even when he turns his attention to the far away or long ago, he relentlessly familiarizes the created landscape in such a way that we wonder at his ability to sustain even a trace of strangeness. Oedipus, he reminds us, was to Freud "the great mythical King," whose name covers "our common wish not to share mom with anyone, not even with dad." Carl's handling of ideas and concepts—evolution, the coming of the messiah, friendship—is at once intimate and minimally oblique, not always comfortable and just a little off-center. To read him is to feel we have, or would be fortunate to have, a friend, but that no matter how well we knew him we'd never quite get to the bottom of him or begin to understand anything quite as he does. He'd never for a moment be inclined to remind us of the gap between us, but we'd feel it, and we'd wonder at his tact in making us feel easy about it.

Carl's idiom is what is sometimes called a plain language, though *plain* doesn't quite get it right. To be sure, there are, in Carl's work, no purple passages, very few swelling cadences or audacious coinages. Typically we get a steady diet of one- and two-syllable words, no one of which we'd need to look up. Every now and then we are brought up short by an abstract formulation—"the field of the never-to-be-embodied"—or a brief, ironically lugubrious sentence—"This Sunday I'm going to lie here quietly and savor the town concerto"—but we're not apt to expect or wait for more extravagant surprises. The stanzas keep coming, now plaintive, now uncertain or playful or reminiscent, occasionally with some gorgeous luster, a soft wind of modest, incontrovertible disillusion at its back. At each turn the words seem to us exact, shaped precisely to the measure of the poet's intent, neither too little nor too much. When he speaks of "love for the truth" we are confident that he will avoid waxing unduly grand or pretentious, that he'll justify his words and bring his modesty to life so that we can feel in the end that we are all of us entitled —occasionally—to speak of the truth. But only if we keep our voices low, our eyes trained patiently on the life before us, our words scrupulous and exact.

Carl's landscape features all of the emotions and all of the big-ticket ideas, but mounted, each of them, on "the smallest scale," and with a wry, wary diffidence, as if the poet knew, somehow, to protect himself from any possibility of delusion, false grandeur, melodramatic exaggeration, unearned despair. As he says, in many poems, in many ways, it's usually good advice to "try something you can handle" and beware of sights, notions, outlying prospects "too far to be seen."

Carl Dennis is the author, thus far, of eight books of poetry. For thirty years, exactly, I have read what Randall Jarrell—in an essay on Marianne Moore—once called those "hard, tender, serious" and playful pages with undiminishing avidity, and I am here to say, not for the first time, what a pleasure it is to anticipate Carl's new work and to revisit the beautifully just, witty, and sometimes heartbreaking poems he has given us.

DEBORAH DIGGES [1999]

"Better," Deborah Digges writes in a magnificent poem called "Akhmatova," "Better we all let go of the lie/ that art can save a life, except perhaps its maker's/ and even then, one might argue/ this is deception."

I begin with these lines because they ring with the sort of hard, troubling, ambivalent yet determined propensity for truth-telling that more and more marks the work of this poet. Of course, we learn, as we read the poems and allow ourselves to be pleasured and troubled and instructed, that the propensity for truth-telling is by no means to be mistaken for the conviction that the poet is in reliable possession of the truth. Even where she utters something that sounds certain, conclusive, something like "Life is a wild undoing!" we can hear in the accents of the poem itself the unspoken under-voice that questions and refuses anything conclusive. Truth-telling, in the work of Deborah Digges, is a habit of mind, a reflex of intelligence, a reaching and correcting, so that truth-telling becomes indistinguishable from listening and looking and feeling and adjusting. What the poet suddenly, unreliably thinks she knows is like a "ringing in the ears," an impression carried on a ceaseless tide of impressions which never gather for good and all on any certain stable shore.

No doubt many readers of the poems of Deborah Digges will regard talk of truth-telling as more than a little beside the point where this poet is concerned. She is not, after all, a poet of ideas, though she is as interested in ideas, in Freud and Marx and Darwin and other such thinkers, as most other first rate poets are apt some of the time to be. And if she does, very often, proceed by interrogation and correction, does sometimes halt

27

the progress of a characteristic poem with "Or let me put it this way," or some such phrase, we know that candor and reflection and setting the record straight are hardly what this poet is all about. It may even be that for some good readers what matters most is not what the poems say so much as what they are, and what they are is musical, skillful, felicitous, but also more than occasionally "fierce," "unpredictable," and even "headlong," as the poet Mark Doty has rightly noted. This is a poetry that can accommodate a line like "How many times I've taken an axe to silence!" without at all seeming lurid or clamoring unduly for our attention, confident as this poet is that even her more modest grace notes will reverberate in our ears and hold us. This is a poetry in which the unexpected turn in a phrase, the suddenly illuminating metaphor, can seem instantly right, not only justifiable but inevitable.

"There is sadness older than its texts," we read in a poem called "Chekov's Darling," "that will outlive the language/ like the lover who takes you by the roots of your hair," and as we take in those lines we see, or think we see, how the strange, unsettling lover's gesture, with its combination of desire and violence, need and violation, is in fact a perfect token of the sensation of tasting and simultaneously being "raised above your pain" that is central to the work of this poet.

Deborah has given us three extraordinary books of poems, and a memoir entitled *Fugitive Spring*. Her work, all of it, is powerfully felt and engaging, marked by a poeticism that is never strained or excessive, never merely elegant, and by an intelligence that is often disarming, capable of regarding its own experience with passionate intensity and with just the necessary measure of grave or amused disinterestedness.

STEPHEN DOBYNS [2001]

Well known, in our town certainly, as the author of the Charlie Bradshaw mystery novels set in our own Saratoga Springs—for novels with titles like *Saratoga Swimmer, Saratoga Bestiary,* and *Dancer with One Leg*—Stephen Dobyns is also the author of several other novels of a very different kind. Yet typically he has read to us, at the Summer Writers' Institute, poems. Stephen is, and for thirty years has been, one of the most interesting and versatile poets in the country, author of many books of poems, from *Concurring Beasts* (which won the Lamont Poetry Prize in 1971) to *The Balthus Poems, Cemetery Nights, Body Traffic,* and a sizeable selected poems called *Velocities.* Poet and novelist, Steve has produced an enormous body of work of an inventiveness and humor matched by very few American writers. Louise Glück, in an article published several years ago in the *American Poetry Review,* made the case for him as one of our most gifted and ambitious contemporary writers, and his work is compelling enough to make the case for itself.

In some ways Steve's poetry is as various as the titles of his books. There are narratives, long and short; there are meditations and *memento moris,* satires and scatological epistles. Often the mood is plaintive or macabre, but just as often the macabre can turn wry and playful. One feels in many of the poems a buoyant theatricality, even where the subject matter runs to loss and death. Though Dobyns' narrator, or speaker, is likely to be—as he once put it—"lost in the country between want to and can't," the casual and meticulous oddity of Steve's images makes us feel hopeful and energetic even where no reasons are offered for optimism of any kind. The writing in the poems is arrestingly crisp, and there is no element of self-pity, evasion or obfuscation. The narratives are distinguished by a remorseless simplicity, though they are, all the while, full of vivid incident and imagistic color. The more sombre lyrics, including some among the brilliant Balthus poems built around works of the great twentieth century painter, achieve density and reflective subtlety without any sacrifice of immediacy or emotional candor.

In all, Steve's poems give accessibility, energy, high risk and pleasure-giving a good name. What kind of pleasure? For one, there is the pleasure in following out the clean lines of an invention that is extravagant without seeming in the least worked up. Note the casual opening of a poem called "Spiritual Chickens":"A man eats a chicken every day for lunch,/ and each day the ghost of another chicken/ Joins the crowd in the dining room." A fine premise, that, requiring for its working through the combination of deadpan delivery and buoyant extrapolation that is a hallmark of Steve's work. The deadpan is the dominant accent of the entire poem, as it is often in Dobyns. The extrapolation comes at the place where the premise is revealed to be the basis for a philosophical or psychological reflection. The turn in "Spiritual Chickens" occurs just after one particular Ghost-chicken at his table begins to act up, and the narrator begins to hop around and flap his arms, and is summarily taken away, "for a cure," prompting this reflection: "Faced with the choice between something odd/ in the world or something broken in his head,/ he opts for the broken head."

Of course we don't quite know, here or in many other Dobyns poems, how to take in the reflection. The tone, after all, is continuous with the deadpan tone used to establish the wild premise, so that what sounds like a "serious" reflection is, may well be, a teaser, laced with irony, a self-canceling form of earnestness.

The irony is not in the least flippant, and there is, one feels, a certain sobering insight within the essentially ironic cast of mind. At whom would the irony be directed here? In part, one supposes, at the author himself, who is relentlessly attracted to deriving insight, apercus, wisdom, from the stuff of his own extravagant, playful invention.

But for all of his instinct for play, for verbal and conceptual mischief, we feel in Steve's work the pressure of a wide experience, even an impulsion from within, so that there is rarely any communicated impression of a poetry merely, skillfully, tossed off. The detachment and control in Dobyns are ever at the service of discovery. When he walks us through what he once called "The City of Missed Chances" and projects our common anxieties onto a dog, "colorful,/ uncertain," who makes "tentative barks at the moon," we accept that we are in the hands of a poet who is up to something gravely serious, though often unable, unwilling, to abandon his appetite for novelty, projection, leaps of wit, the grotesque, the improbable, the farcical. Yet the effect of all of this invention is apt, much of the time, to resemble "a hammer sinking chains into concrete,/ . . .doors slamming and locking one after another." This poet, maybe more often than even he would allow, delivers blows that sink deep.

CAROLYN FORCHÉ [1999]

In 1983, my friend Terence Diggory wrote about what was then Carolyn Forché's new book, *The Country Between Us*, in a piece that begins as follows: "The honors showered upon Carolyn Forché during her brief career so far do not compensate for the misunderstanding that has accompanied them." That misunderstanding had to do with the very character of Carolyn's work, and some aspect of that misunderstanding has persisted to this day, discernible even in the praises showered upon Carolyn's more recent work, *The Angel of History*.

At the heart of Carolyn's poetry, no doubt about it, is an effort to bear witness to important events and tribulations that mark the experience of this century—in Latin America, in central Europe, and elsewhere. No reader of Carolyn's work can fail to note her interest in the lives of other people, and in the political conflicts that have loomed so large in many of those lives. On the basis of these obvious facts, many have determined to read Carolyn as primarily a political poet and to demand of her work the kinds of affirmation that are not typically on offer in the poems.

Though Carolyn has written of El Salvador and Auschwitz, of Vietnam and the Nazi occupation of Paris, she has written not to establish an easy solidarity with victims but to bear witness in a more arduous sense—to evoke, to remember, to meditate, to dramatize: these have been Carolyn's aims. What she has sought to dramatize is, has always been, a deep and evolving personal investment in the lives of others, and also a deep and uncertain sense of the dark places in our hearts that keep us apart from others, however much we may wish to erase distance and to sacramentalize those moments when separateness seems to have been overcome. The strenuousness of Carolyn's effort, the striving and hoping and straining and only intermittent exhilaration it affords, all of these are manifests of the tentativeness of her enterprise, of the gap that separates Carolyn's poetry utterly from the programmatic and the uplifting.

Of course it is also more than a little misleading to speak of Carolyn's work as a unitary phenomenon. After all, her first book, *Gathering the Tribes*, was, or seemed, a largely autobiographical volume, with poems variously focused on the poet's Slovak ancestry, on her own sexual awakening, and on various other largely personal matters. *The Country Between Us* is, by comparison, a work with a more public dimension, its famous poems including those which detail events Carolyn witnessed in Central America. The contrast is clear, though in saying so, I reflect that even in this justly celebrated second book the effort is principally to think about the struggle of the imagination to record and master its experience, to resist the seductions of sentimentality and sensationalism, to remain scrupulous, attentive, decent, humanly intact. Is this political poetry? Well, if it is, it points the way to what political poetry can be, and reminds us of what it needn't be.

So, too, is *The Angel of History* an exemplary and yet very different sort of book, invested in a vision of political conflict, but in no way an effort to strike edifying postures. As many of us know, who have read this wonderful book over and again for ourselves, and heard Carolyn read from it here, it is a book of memories, of voices and fragmentary stories, involving persons whose lives were shaped by the second world war. Within the book, the Holocaust and Hiroshima are singled out as two defining events of our century, but a great many events are handled in elegiac fragments that run from a phrase or a line to a few stanzas. The effect of the poem is like nothing else I know, and if that sounds extravagant, well, I don't know how else to say what has been the truth of my response to Carolyn's work ever since I heard her read it. Some combination of bleakness and intensity is what I have heard and felt in this poetry, intimations of crossed, unstable identities, a striving to speak in and through a multiplicity of voices without entirely losing one's own voice. Though there has been some resistance, here and there, to the music of Carolyn's book-length poem, it seems to me a major work of the imagination.

CAROLYN FORCHÉ [2000]

"For years," Carolyn Forché says in one of the beautiful new poems she has just given us, "For years I have opened my eyes and not known where I was." That is very like the note we have lately come to associate with Carolyn's stance, a note of wonder, of more or less steady disorientation, even sometimes of stunned amazement, though always too there is correction, the shifting and squinting and taking stock that bring things briefly back into focus, the progressive feeling backwards and forwards that is this poet's favored, habitual process of vision and re-vision. "Objects in the room grew small grew large again," she says in that same new poem, so that, for all of the poet's urgency about what happened once upon a time, for all of her loving attention to detail, the colorings of surfaces and windows, the suitcases of clippings, the smeared walls, the graves and deaths and diggings and sequesterings, we are drawn again and again to the poet's ever repeating act of vision and re-vision. Even what is apparently true and actual and felt in such a poem participates in what feels like a perpetual dredging up of not-quite-certain or fully confirmable realities. The flesh and blood son who is substance and emblem of the poem called "Blue Hour" is yet, also, "this one who had come toward me all my life," as much a fate as a person, a becoming at least as much as a being, a child, as Carolyn says, "already disappearing into a man," so that she knows and does not know what she has made, what she loves.

In another new poem called "Nocturne" we begin at the beginning with the stark question, "What happened?", and though we then circle for pages round and round several pregnant, almost palpable somethings that happened, and take them in as surely and feelingly as the poet who holds us securely in her hands will allow, we are never quite confident we can distinguish between appearance and fact, dream and remembrance, fear and mourning. When, late in the poem, another question is invoked, and the answer given—"no, he could not have done it"—we feel nevertheless that the more probable answer would be, must be, yes, of course, he did it, for if he had not done it, had not tied a rope around his throat and found himself, as the poet says, "in the coroner's arms," then there would be no need to ask, and deny, and circle back, and play over the attendant circumstance, and register again the overpowering sense of loss. But we are never entirely sure about any of this, about how to put together with the dear one apparently departed. . . another one also apparently departed and the nagging reminder that she who remembers and grieves is determined to be altogether she who remembers and grieves.

Of course, the poet also insists upon the idea that there is a "beginning of life after death," and on the prospect of what she calls "a coherent life." And so these new poems are always remembering and determining and correcting. Equilibrium is at best tentative, but it is, throughout, real because necessary, desirable.

The remarkable thing—one remarkable thing—about the new poems of Carolyn Forché is that they aim at every instant of their unfolding to be deeply felt acts of remembering and, at the same time, voyagings out into uncharted and unmasterable waters, so that introspection and discovery are part of a single reflex, and what is there to be recovered can never be entirely sufficient to the hungry soul.

But of course there is more to say—more that we have not the time to say—of these new poems, which you are about to hear, and we cannot fail, if only in a part of a single long sentence, to remember that Carolyn has already been through several drastically different stages in a career that has progressed from intimate autobiography in her first book to the more obviously public and political dimension of *The Country Between Us* and onto the elegiac, often fragmentary, forays into history, the retrievals and meditations and voice-shiftings of the volume *The Angel of History*. Carolyn is, as we well know, one of our permanent and indispensable poets.

CAROLYN FORCHÉ [2001]

Though she is—believe me—just now entering upon middle age, there is nothing middling about the recent poetry of Carolyn Forché. Carolyn's early gift for musical phrasing, for capturing emotions in sharp images, for suggesting—without underlining—signal shifts in the attitude of the speaker, her precise yet fluent mastery of idiom and incident: all of that early gift has been sustained in the work of the last decade, but transformed more or less utterly in the uses and effects to which that gift is directed. Carolyn was never a writer given to what Yeats called, ironically, "pretty plumage," though she has been willing to write beautifully, to elect not merely the right word or image but the word with the greatest possible vividness and dramatic justification. The transformation, so obvious to us now, has much to do with a quality not easily defined. To say, as a beginning, that there is in the work of the last decade a greater or more intense degree of subjectivity, is perhaps to suggest that earlier the poetry lacked subjectivity, which is palpably, totally misleading. But nowhere in the early work is there, or not with any persistence, the "black storms of dream" that dominate much of the newer poems, the alertness to apparition, intimations of soul, potential messages from "a secret self," attempts to identify and interpret "a secret that stands apart from every secret."

The poems of Carolyn Forché have always been, we may say, deeply subjective, bearing with them in every trace the marks of a turbulent inner life. But Carolyn has lately discovered, or so it would seem, a persistent connection between every simple thing the poet observes and the "spiral" of her own being. More and more, as we read the new poems, soon to appear in a volume entitled *Blue Hour*, and hear Carolyn read them, we are alert to the accent of inquisition, of troubled and hopeful interrogation. The bond between object and meaning is now less certain than it was, the "net of purpose" more tentative, more widely cast, and with less certain prospect of gathering its contents into a secure, determinate, compact catch.

The remarkable thing about this transformation is that the new work is no less precise in its handling of metaphor and idiom and texture than the earlier poems. There are, in Carolyn's newer poems, abundant particulars to discipline the dreaming subjectivity and to hold it to a world out there. Present and past are accorded their distinctive shapes and contents. Details proliferate, climb up out of an obscurity, insinuate themselves into our consciousness, briefly set down tentative roots, only to dissolve, leaving with us a residue we cannot dispel. Resolute as the poet is to insist that she has mainly fragments to offer, "something broken and personal," "pieces of language" or memory or projected desire torn "from something larger," it is a palpable universe we feel ourselves to be immersed in as we give ourselves to Carolyn's poems, though "the breath of the invisible" is ever there, pressing the poet to acknowledge its ghostly presence, pressing us to yield, to breathe in an ether at once exhilarating and forbidding, a temptation, as Carolyn writes, "beyond the grasp of thought."

In the end, whatever is obscured in Carolyn's poems is only "imperfectly erased" and that which is "vanished" seems, if only intermittently, present again, somehow strangely "visible on earth," and on the page. The tendency of the poet to drift away, to get lost, to interrogate the protean and the boundless, is checked, set in tension with the alternative impulse to remember, record, tally up, though, as the poet says, in these precincts, "x does not equal." That formulation, "x does not equal," is here very precise and haunting. It sharply captures the essential operant reflex, though it cannot give us—no compact formulation can—the quality of the rapt, inquiring, delicately hovering voice that belongs to Carolyn alone. That voice—we'll hear it together in a few moments—moves us to note that the mind moving here among its impressions and fragments and desires is in touch with an order of being—I wish I knew what exactly to call it—we are privileged only to glimpse and, now and then, with Carolyn's help, very cautiously to enter. Carolyn is a poet of "enchanted depths," and her music communicates perfectly the precarious, unappeasable character of her experience.

LOUISE GLÜCK [1994]

Louise Glück is the author of six books which represent one of the major achievements in late 20th century writing. Early associated—though mistakenly, it now seems—with the confessional poets and their relentless appetite for unpleasantness and self-exposure, she has developed an increasingly original, harsh, sometimes forbidding manner, as notable for its moral fierceness as for its resistance to most forms of adornment or expressive excess. Indeed, her recent Pulitzer Prize-winning volume, *The Wild Iris*, offers poems shaped in the medium of prayer and brushed by the ghostly consciousness familiar to readers of her previous volumes. It is no wonder that, in reviews and essays on her work, the most frequent epithets include words like *spare, somber, anguished, skeletal*. The critic Helen Vendler has written that Louise engages reality in "the style of the rock, rather than the stream of consciousness," that she confronts us with "a precipitate, a residue, from life's fluidity," an "almost posthumously gentle" or trance-like expression.

No one would deny for a moment the claims of reality in Louise's poems, however sharply formalized the utterance. She writes, in often contradictory or ambivalent terms, about love, death, marriage, sexual passion, motherhood, mourning, even — and increasingly—about the vicissitudes of religious feeling. But these are not, for Louise, subjects in the usual sense. For all the named emotion and raw simplicities, the poems move relentlessly toward abstraction, the mythic and the archetypal. The male character who suffers his encounter with a sexual other is more, and less, than this woman's husband, or that woman's lover. He is Man, and what we know of him is no more than what may be said of his kind in general. When we find ourselves locked in the perspective of a child, it is childhood we confront, with its attendant characteristic features of vulnerability or incomprehension. For all the individuality of the floral emblems in *The Wild Iris,* for all our sense that one voice can not be mistaken for another, our attention, our interest, is drawn to the predicament of mortality in general, the baffled intimation of a higher power in the face of which individuality is of little consequence.

The really remarkable thing, given the tendency of Louise's work to turn away from specific details or to convert them instantly into emblems, is that no dramatic urgency is lost thereby. For all of their measured perfections, Louise's poems have a haunted air, and they speak frequently with an intensity —now hot, now cold—that is as harrowing for a reader as for the persona who speaks. At the heart of this poetry, with its hungers and its anguish, its mournfulness and sometimes breathtaking austerities, is a perpetual wrestling with questions of identity and union and remembering. But through it all we hear, in the fatedness of the logic, in the always defeated longing for consolation or transport, the steady accent of Renunciation. This will to renounce is the true voice of feeling in Louise Glück's poetry, and the mark of the spiritual exertion that so distinguishes her work.

LOUISE GLÜCK [2000]

Recently, in an issue of *The New Yorker*, there appeared a new poem by Louise Glück entitled "Time." Like many of the poems she has been writing in the last few years, "Time" is at once tentative and inexorable, beautiful and terrifying. It is a poem of remembrance and renunciation, in which the intuitive knowledge of children—of one child at least—is expressed as: "best to remain unconscious." And yet the determination, as Louise says, "to live in the spirit," is also central in this poem, and inevitably calls to mind the many other poems in which Louise has wrestled with spirit, fearful often about the erosion of the absolute, drawn, as she tells us, to Abstraction and alert to the disquieting possibility that an apt word for "spirit" is "void," as in *vacant*, as in *nothing*.

But the memories that haunt Louise's recent poem are not nothing, though they revolve about a preoccupation with the passage of time, the impress of dreams, the absence of signs sufficient to justify the poet's determination to live in the spirit. Reading such a poem, we are moved again and again by intimations of a lived life, by small details that sharply if only briefly convey the flavor of things, the ways dogs sleep on a child's bed, or a mother is summoned to a sickbed by the ringing of a bell. Always in Louise's work we are struck by her inveterate habit of converting everything into emblems, actions into myth, while sacrificing no whit of dramatic urgency, no sense of speaking out of an experience that is as real and felt and substantial as experience can be. And so we are not surprised that the poem entitled "Time" should seem to us the intimate record of a lived experience even as it seems a poem about remembrance and loss, about the growth of consciousness and the awareness of time as "a weight that couldn't be moved." Louise says in another poem that she "was trying to be/ a witness not a theorist," but of course the distinction doesn't quite get at the strange doubleness of Louise's characteristic perspective, her almost theoretical rigor and her scrupulous attention to what makes her own life singular and yet, however improbably, an emblem of the common life.

At the Library of Congress this past spring I heard Louise read eight or more of the poems that will appear in her next book, and I said to her, as simply and truthfully as I could, that those poems left me feeling happy and inconsolable, like nothing else I'd lately heard or read. Why happy? Louise asked, apparently satisfied with my *inconsolable*. Because, I answered, the poems are so utterly, perfectly terrifying, so beautiful in their extremity of anguish, so that they make almost everything else seem frivolous.

To be sure, we have long found in Louise's work a strenuous exertion of soul, a hunger to exist outside of conventional deception, a willingness to explore "human faithlessness." But we hear in the newer work little of the plaintiveness and accusation that have so moved us before. It is as if the poet had left those sentiments largely behind her, reaching for something even darker, more stern and forbidding, something that raises to an even higher pitch of cold intensity her old sense of fatedness. I don't know that we'd want any longer to insist on the presence—not in the new poems, at any rate—of what one very astute reader called an "almost posthumously gentle" expression, but the word "posthumous" remains compelling, almost inescapable as we make our way through poems as undefended as any American poems we know.

LOUISE GLÜCK [2001]

By now it is a commonplace to say that Louise Glück is a poet of austerities, that she does with a few words, a phrase, an occasional detail or metaphor what others strive, strain, fail to accomplish with more. Her most recent book, *The Seven Ages*, is in some respects the most spare and terrifying of her nine volumes, a book, yes, austere and inexorable, more than occasionally forbidding, and yet, never fatally cold, never poised with that perfection of achieved indifference the poet herself seems now and again to desire. *The Seven Ages* is, no doubt about it, a book of leave-takings, a coming-to-terms with that which cannot change or be changed. But it is, not at all oddly, for all of its determined retreat to the "closed" and the "fixed," the "formal" and the ritualistic, a book of poems quick with life, quick even with the stabbing recognition of life "never completely lived," of desire unsatisfiable and desiring still.

How often, sustained, flattened by one of Louise's poems do we ask, not for the first time, how it is possible, how less can be more, small things large, a spare detail suddenly appear to us strange, meaning loom into sight without the customary heaving and hoisting we associate with a poetry of dark intensities. We note how, in this work, and more frequently than ever before in Louise, abstraction is blooded, terms like "tranquil" and "beautiful" and "dutiful" not merely serviceable but loaded with an inexpressable weight of longing or rejection. And we note, too, that the compression in Louise's work never feels willed, never seems a coy withholding of magical potencies. This is a poetry not particularly avid to exercise its lyricism but, perhaps in spite of itself, painfully beautiful, fluent in the languages of day dream and sleepwalk, trance and twilight. The sense of the past is ever present in these poems, the past itself shifting and eddying, as the poet says, all too aware of the fact that the past "no longer exists," but willing to practice the arts of retrieval, if only to taste the loss of what was, to savor the sensation of doing without. Did the lovers once lie together in one another's arms, the poet or her surrogate will ask, moved by "shadows on the dark grass"? To ask is perhaps to see, as she writes, "their shattered hearts mended again, as in life of course/ they never will be." There is nothing like a triumphal note in that "of course," that "never," though there is, unmistakeably, a certain pleasure, or pride, in yielding to the facts, the irrecoverable "something" that cannot be controlled. So much, in Louise's book, falls into that, belongs to the domain of gone, too late, she missed, passing, never. And everywhere there are vivid tokens of that passing, brief but miraculously substantial, captured moments of a past before the passing, of a past already known to be over, a past infecting, inspiring, in Louise's words, "the dream of the mind," which is, however sad, and whatever the felt "inertia" of the present moment, a "dream of the future."

This is not, I think, the time to enumerate the captured moments, to recite the substantial tokens, as Louise no doubt will recite them, or many of them, in a few moments. But I must say, in almost closing here, that Louise's new book seems to me the single bravest book of poems by any contemporary writer I know, confronting as it does, and with an almost unbearable though disciplined urgency, sentiments, fears, intimations, almost no one else will name, let alone summon with the full weight of her intelligence. Louise's book is haunted by emptiness, the incomprehensible, the too-well understood, the wrong turn, pleasure recalled, and pleasure alive still in forms seductive or exhausting. Throughout the book we hear the sound of anguish, but it is, or seems to us to be, an anguish mastered, ordered, with an order that is never fully settled, always gesturing at a completion, a final ordering the poet knows to be not possible, and therefore unutterably compelling. The world in Louise's poems is at once harsher and clearer than what we customarily call life itself, and the facts, or what she would have us take to be the facts, become newly real, invested as they are with the power of this poet's strict, relentless summoning.

BARRY GOLDENSOHN [1999]

Barry Goldensohn is one of our least predictable, most playfully allusive and intellectually rewarding poets. Among his best work are poems of considerable philosophic breadth and poems of ranging historical imagination. Others are short, stabbing lyrics, alternately plaintive, brusque and witty. In some of his work one hears the under-voice of a rich music, but more typically his is a hard-bitten idiom that sharply reflects the complication and intensity of his thought. Though occasionally he works with a surprisingly variegated palette, most often he eschews colorful effects, opting instead for a spare and riddling penetration.

In short, no one of his poems can suggest the range of his accomplishment. A poet who is often intricate and elusive, and not much given to wearing the gaudier sentiments on his sleeve, he is yet, unmistakably, a poet of emotion, by turns tender and severe, susceptible to nostalgia and unforgiving dispassion. The author of stark and plaintive elegies, he is also drawn, with surprising frequency, to the love poem and the miniaturized family saga.

The voices in Goldensohn's poems are by turns poetic and colloquial. The devices, such as they are, are casually accommodated, as if nothing could seem to this poet more natural, more like an odd piece of clothing thrown on and as easily discarded. He can open a poem on "Nôtre Dame de Paris" with a near ecstatic exclamation—"The great radial sweeps of rose window,/ the towers"—and descend at once to a biting, ironic take on the resident preacher's "potent/ tenor sentences." Often confiding, even confessional, he is nonetheless alert to the falsity and self-deception that come with "loose talk" and "theatrical emotion."

Unlike most other poets of his generation, Goldensohn writes frankly out of a deeply obstructed activity of mind. Honoring the formal imperatives demanded by the dominant aesthetic of high modernism, he honors as well the messy origins of a living poem. He wants his poems to seem self-sufficient, sovereign, but also to imply the irrelevances that acted upon their making. That is why, when we read a first-rate Goldensohn poem, we feel that it moves elegantly on the brink of untidiness. He gives us a poise that is wonderful because it is unstable, a sense of focus that holds us because it threatens to slip away or wander off. We admire most in his work the mark of a restless and large intelligence, a capacity for wonder that is never very far from a capacity to register and absorb pain. In such contrary qualities may be found the key to Goldensohn's singularity.

No poet of Barry Goldensohn's generation is at once so accomplished and so little celebrated. I believe that this has everything to do with the fact that his books have been published by very small presses in very small editions. But the poems continue to come on, and those of us who have found our way to them must say, with this reader, that Barry Goldensohn has found a way to riddle and unlock the heart.

JORIE GRAHAM [1997]

About most poets worth discussing it is easy to say the wrong thing—say, to cite the features of an early poem and pretend they are present in later, very different poems; to mistake the ideas contained in a poem for its point or purpose. How often do we as readers leap to unwarranted conclusions—even with poets notable for their single-mindedness—by paying too much attention to a resonant phrase or a vivid image, by missing the irony in a stanza that looked like earnestness itself but that we had reason nonetheless to suspect?

About the work of Jorie Graham, which is anything but single-minded, it is perhaps easier to say the wrong thing than about any other poet of her generation. She has written a great many poems, some of them quite long and difficult. She has seemed to undertake, with each new book she has published, something new. Where once, in speaking of her as a philosophical poet, one knew more or less what kinds of things she would typically do and not do, she now inspires some readers to speak of her as an essentially descriptive poet, resolved "to remain, linguistically, on the material plane." The critic Helen Vendler, whose commitment to the work of Jorie Graham is unwavering and exemplary, nonetheless finds herself reaching, grasping, not always successfully, for words that can do justice to the poet's shiftings and subversions. She is right, surely, to associate a dimension of Graham's lyric with the "austere" and "renunciatory," but she can't help also using such terms as "intense and lavish" to get at Graham, who at one moment calls to Vendler's mind "the Whitmanian ecstatic sublime" but at another reminds her of the more "intimate" vision of so utterly different a poet as Emily Dickinson.

All of which is to say that, with Jorie Graham, we come face to face with a poetry of enormous range and ambition. Can we say, with some confidence, what the poetry, most of it, is principally about? One poet says that it is about the search for salvation, another that it is a quest to find out who or what we are. Some say it is about what the poem as a form of knowledge can know. A recent reviewer says the poems are about "the limits of subjectivity in relation to 'objects of desire,'" but that they are also about "the question of faith." Vendler asserts that what is primary in the latest poems is "the dissolution of meaning into unmeaning."

But all such reflections, however helpful, fail to convey what is essential about the poetry of Jorie Graham. True, from the time of her first book she has been concerned with questions of meaning and with what we see when we look, analyze and penetrate. But there is a strange and unfamiliar dimension to Graham's reflections on these questions. What, she asks, do we miss when we think, associate, let one thing remind us of another, reason carefully on the basis of available evidence, order our perceptions? It's strange, or so it seems to me, that a poet who has thought so rigorously, who knows so very much about ideas and about thinking, should have been, for so long, so skeptical about thoughts, about ideas, about connections and resemblances. And it is strange, no doubt about it, that such a poet is more and more attracted to the random, the shapeless, the indeterminate, the impermanent. Here, after all, as in a recent poem called "The Angel of Self-Knowledge," is a poet who suggests that our effort to find some truth, wherever we search, possibly "doesn't matter, since we can't tell the difference."

But the truth is in the experience of Jorie Graham's poems, not in the various statements they make or in their "gusts" of meaning and unmeaning. To read these poems is to feel how much everything matters to this poet, how entirely she insists that nothing be lost on her, that no distortion or desire be unrecorded, that no sound of "sandals on stone," no "hissing of cars passing," no shade or color or light be ignored. Does she suppose that, in the end, all will be revealed, that by opening her self to everything she will arrive at a final, singular, incontrovertible truth? No such suggestion is to be found in Jorie Graham's poems, but we do hear, again and again, some version of the question: "Did I ask all the questions?" Can I be sure I have "been in this scene deeply enough?"

To be in the presence of so fierce a demand for adequacy and attentiveness is to sense how much there is for all of us to know, how alternately exhilarating and troubling it can be to reach for understanding without any prospect of completion. *The Dream of the Unified Field*—the title of Jorie Graham's Pulitzer-Prize-winning selected poems—can be a beautiful dream, a dream of possession, wholeness and control, but this is one poet for whom desire is always greater than what can be possessed. She is also a poet for whom an "intense openness to sensory experience," as Peter Sacks once put it, is marked by an equally intense and indisputably rare commitment to thinking.

ROBERT HASS [1994]

I remember very clearly the first time I read Robert Hass. It was twenty-five years ago, and there were three perfectly beautiful and moving poems, offered to my magazine *Salmagundi* and shortly afterward published there at the front of our twelfth issue. I looked back at those poems earlier this week, and I marveled again at their assurance and maturity, at their confident movement from political statement to historical reverie and sheer physical immediacy—from lines like "Washington was calm, murderous, neoclassical./ More lies than cherry trees and nothing changed" to very different lines, like "A furious, dun-colored mallard knows my lust/and swims across the edges of the marsh/ where the dead cod surface/and their flaccid bellies bob." For all the occasional turmoil and anger in those early poems, one saw even then the extraordinary poise, the disciplined reaching for still hours beyond desire, beyond contempt or disappointment.

One has felt in Bob's work throughout the years a meditative calm and a capacity for reappraisal that are the mark of a robust moral imagination. Though the early works continue to satisfy and surprise, one is stuck by the changes through which this poet has taken himself, by the deepening of the inquiry he has long conducted.

Bob has always been associated with the west coast, with the landscape and history and legends of California, but he is about as far as a poet can get from a narrow regional provincialism. His poetry draws heavily on Asian and on European sources. You find in one poem an emanation of delicate images, as from Japanese haiku, in another poem the gaudy music of Stevens, or the quick stress lines of William Carlos Williams, or the prosaic accents of social engagement and self-reflection reminiscent of Czeslaw Milosz, whose work Bob has brilliantly translated into English. Often a poet given to praise and pleasure and openness very much in the American grain, he has also displayed some uneasiness with hedonism and the easy avoidance of limits to which many American writers are attached. Never a poet to put a willfully grim face on things, he has known how to play without forgetting exigency and power and loss. The western expanses of comfort and warmth, where—as he has it—"The lemons were yellowing/ and no other task presented itself"— routinely beckon in Bob's poems, and so too do we hear—now blurred, now sharp and unmistakable—the cry of grieving, restlessness and loss. For every long meadow and "Something like hilarity" there is "the maimed figure of the god," the well fouled, the crops withered.

Bob's most recent volume, *Human Wishes*, contains some of his best work, and includes poems of assertion, highly suggestive prose vignettes, and a number of long meditative lyrics that are among the finest works of his generation. Those longer poems especially remind us of Bob's deep investment in words as sacred incarnations of the world, but they remind us too that for him there is always the haunting thought that language is neither complete nor sufficient, just as beauty is neither an adequate compensation for pain nor reliably ours for the asking. The richness of Bob's relationship to sufficiency and denial, consolation and grieving, is perfectly captured in a few words from his poem "Sunrise," in which he confronts "the table set for abstinence." There, it seems to me, is an emblem of a poetry simultaneously alert to every brightness and committed to telling every kind of hard truth.

SEAMUS HEANEY [1992]

"Is it any wonder," Seamus Heaney asks in a poem called "Terminus," "when I thought/ I would have second thoughts?" No wonder, to be sure, for us, faithful readers of poems marked, from the first, by many varieties of second thoughts, misgivings, self-doubts, recoils and conditionals. A lover of exuberance and release, an admirer of the "wandering voice" and a poetry of "pure play," Seamus is, at the same time, a stern moralist—stern at least in self-interrogation and in scrupulous self-correction. This is a poet adept, as he has often intimated, at "suffering the limit of each claim." And what is that limit, we may ask, if not that margin where doubt encroaches upon assertion, where the road robustly taken suddenly looks like a road shadowed by "dreaded omen" or "evil eye."

Seamus's poetry is very much in touch with myth and legend, but it is not a poetry infatuated with magic or tempted by superstition. It is ever in search of plausible epiphanies and clarifications, but wary of grand or blinding illuminations. The world, in Seamus's poetry, can be a great good place, but it is also a place of abrasions and resignations, where, to be fully alive, is to feel oneself tested, one's ordinary tendency to moderation and "decency" at least intermittently subjected to derision. The poet himself, so he suggests, may not be—or not always—the one "whose boat will lift when the cloudburst happens," but he will more than occasionally stand his modest ground, resist the bland imperatives to equivocate, swerve, apologize.

Even in his great 1975 volume, *North*, we were let in on a dark, unresolvable tension in Seamus's outlook, a tension reflected in the marrow of his diction and the rhythm of his speech. In *North* the tension was felt in the disparity between the tendency to bluntness and astringency, on the one hand, and the pervasive, unimpeachable fellow-feeling everywhere apparent even in poems notable for what the poet calls their "iron composition" and their resistance to nostalgia.

Of course there are many varieties of tension in Seamus's work, and the tenor of the most memorable poems in *North* is quite different from the tenor of the major poems in *Station Island* or *The Haw Lantern*. In section four of the long sequence called "Clearances" the tenor is retrospective, anecdotal, albeit with a formal stringency imposed by the sonnet form, but the tension is harder to name. Clearly it has something to do with a diction that is at once precise and yet surprising in the liberties it affords itself. Clearly, too, the tension is reflected in the poet's dual commitment to truth-telling, on the one hand, and to the tender, humane retrospection that naturally informs a sequence written in memory of the poet's mother.

We register the tension most sharply in the poet's handling of the word "betrayal," where the word designates the poet's willingness to go along with his mother's fear of affectation and her aversion to sophistication or elegance, in short to the artfulness and refinements of the poet himself. And so the poet would, as he says, "naw and aye/ And decently relapse into the wrong/ Grammar which kept us allied and at bay." Charming, and not a little disturbing, that clinching "allied and at bay," but not quite so disturbing and unforgiving as the earlier words, "So I governed my tongue/ In front of her, a genuinely well-/ adjusted adequate betrayal/ of what I knew better." Nothing so sharply captures, I think, the poet's dual commitments, his inveterate, compulsive gift for second thoughts, his deep misgivings, even about his own command of language and idiom, as that line naming the "genuinely well-/ adjusted adequate betrayal."

Was ever the genuine so well and authentically matched with the idea of betrayal as it is in Seamus's poem? Was ever the word "adequate" so entirely a concession to frailty, the "well-adjusted" so bluntly an admission of an ordinary gift for trimming and accommodation? We feel, in such a poem, the war within the poet, his struggle to be decent and better than decent, to own up while doing his best not to unduly wound or confound, his delicate efforts at balance, charity and proportion tested by a contrary instinct to expose, to estrange himself and his reader from the familiar and the comfortable, to resist sleepwalk and every variant of the folded lie.

Seamus Heaney has helped us to understand, more than any poet we know, the meaning of the struggle to identify "right action" and to offer an "uncompromised report" of one's own motives and experience. No poet has given us poems at once so tenderly responsive to the ordinary life we lead and, at the same time, so alert to the several "grammar(s) of imperatives" that make of the good life a constant test. Can I be equal, will I be equal, have I been equal—so Seamus's poems would seem in their many ways to ask—equal to what is demanded of me if I am to think well of myself? With no trace of merely "adequate" self-justification, with no posturing displays of moral rectitude, Seamus's poems represent the most powerful interrogation of our common life that we have had in the last quarter of the twentieth century.

RICHARD HOWARD [1994]

Richard Howard is of course one of this country's most distinguished men of letters, a critic of remarkable erudition, generosity and subtlety; a translator, from French to English, of an extraordinary variety and number of books; and a Pulitzer-prize winning poet whose many volumes are among the most vital and original in all of American poetry. It is no secret that Richard's name has long been associated with developments in the form of the dramatic monologue, and that his famous book, *Untitled Subjects*, features an extraordinary cast of nineteenth century characters, from John Ruskin to Giachino Rossini and Mrs. William Morris. But equally seductive and memorable are Richard's two part inventions, his dialogues involving the likes of Hart Crane and W.H. Auden, or the long narratives of the volume *No Traveller*, or the eulogistic meditations and memoirs that Richard has read to us in recent years at this institute.

I've said before that Richard's poems astonish, enlighten and delight, and now that I've read Richard's new book, *Like Most Revelations*, I can say it again, with renewed conviction. They astonish because they speak in many different voices, range fearlessly from idiom to idiom, sentiment to sentiment, and create opportunities for invention undreamt of by most other poets. The poems enlighten because they have complex things to tell us about people and the past, and are so generous in their inquisitions as to make us eager and curious where before we were merely earnest and dutiful. The poems delight because they are at once playful and severe, theatrical and intimate, confiding and arch—they delight by showing us how to be witty without being superficial. Reading Richard's poems, one hears echoes from, and variations upon, the literary tradition of the west, from Browning and Walter Scott to Henry James and Walt Whitman. One delights in the presence of those who have shaped our sense of the past, and one delights also in the dramatized inadequacy of memory, or language, to reclaim entirely what is at once eternally seductive and irretrievable.

Richard Howard has written so well in so many different kinds of forms that it has always seemed impossible to identify any single characteristic work or mode. Reading in the new book I was tempted, again, to select one of the brilliant dramatic monologues as quintessential Howard, particularly the poem built around Isadora Duncan, or the strange poem that is partly an imagined letter from the painter Pierre Bonnard to Matisse. But there are also the satirical poems, the two-part invention on Robert Frost and Wallace Stevens, the moving elegies for friends like David Kalstone and James Boatwright. And I thought, as I have in the past, that if there is a key to Richard's singular success as a poet, it is his capacity to tell or to suggest stories without ever descending to illustration. Richard's poems are typically involved—deeply involved—in voice, incident, conflict, juxtaposition, in what, taken together, we call anecdotage. But they are never merely anecdotal, any more than they are merely playful or breezily satiric or merely literary. Their charm and their challenge lie in their refusal to be altogether intelligible, in their resistance to being quite as accessible and inviting as they sometimes seem. Perhaps I shouldn't, but I do take the Howard persona quite seriously when he says in "Homage" that "One writes in the end....not to say something but Not to say something." Or when he offers that there are "no ideas but in nothing." Such teasing formulations are perhaps a little forbidding, suggesting as they may that when we read a Howard poem we are entertained by what are after all not much more than supersensible soap bubbles. But one understands why the poet should wish now and then to forbid our becoming too utterly absorbed in his poems, too comfortable in the embrace even of his most dauntingly intricate, if never less than pleasing creations. For, as he says, "It is difficult/ to get rid of people once you have given them/ too much pleasure—particularly those/ who are convinced that they possess a key/ and will not rest until they have arranged/ whatever you wrote into one big lock."

Well, with Richard's poems we are pleased, we are often charmed, we confess it freely; we persist in feeling grateful and absorbed, we crave yet further stories and figures, and most of all the voices with their insidious accents and reticences and indiscretions. But we are instructed, chastened: we acknowledge no key, seek no lock. In the poems of Richard Howard we celebrate, as Oscar Wilde had it, "the transient gladness of color," "the whole sphere of feeling, the perfect cycle of thought."

RICHARD HOWARD [1997]

In a fourteen-part poem called "Compulsive Qualifications" included in the 1976 volume *Fellow Feelings*, Richard Howard answers questions put to him by—what to call him—a younger man, a lover, traveling companion, persistent interlocutor. The questions, Richard's inventions, of course, are themselves wonderful, beginning with "Richard, May I Ask a Question? What is an Episteme?" and going on to "Richard, may I ask you something? Is Poetry Involved with Evil?" and "Richard, May I Ask A Horrible Question? Isn't it Painful When Two Men Make Love Together?"

Long-time readers of Richard Howard's poems will perhaps find the expected in his first effort to answer that last "horrible" question, when he provides a "horrible" answer, namely, "When/ Two men make love apart, that is the most painful." Of course, he knows, as he goes on to say, that the question actually intends something else, intends a concern with what he calls "engineering," "architecture," "bodies" and "parts." And the truth is that, as a poet, Richard is often interested in bodies, in seduction and the engineering of pleasure. So playful is his exploration of this realm that we sometimes, occasionally, forget that it is under-written by a deep interest in the way bodies work, the way they give, sustain and absorb sensation. He knows what there is to know about what he calls "breaking and entering," about the relation between "pain" and "electricity." He knows that, as he says, "everyone's flesh is opaque/to the feelings of others," that "A given body takes time, like a good burglar,/ and cleans up after itself."

But he knows also many other kinds of things, about the cosmic and the impermanent, about the manifold ways of achieving "the unlived life," about the relation between "abstraction" and universals, individuality and resemblance. He is, one might say almost in spite of himself, a philosophical poet with a novelist's interest in character and a singular gift for converting the playful to the serious, the eccentric particular to the general, the daydream to reality.

Richard Howard has won the Pulitzer Prize in poetry, was Poet Laureate of New York State, and is the author of an immensely learned and brilliant critical study of our poetry, entitled *Alone With America*. No one interested in literature will fail to have read several of his many translated works, including books by Gide, Foucault, Barthes and Colette.

But it is, of course, his own poetry that will continue most to delight us, for its wit and its color, its susceptibility to the dark emotions and the light, its obscenity and obliquity. There is much to say about the sheer variety of Richard's work, its copiousness and multiple virtuosities, but who can do it justice in a brief introduction? The critic James Longenbach has celebrated Richard's ability to combine openness and formal rigor, his refusal to accept the distinction between "excellence and ecstasy"—as if, Richard has written, "the one had to, or could, preclude the other." Just so, we want to say of Richard that he is a poet not merely, not alone, of dramatic monologues, but a poet whose gift encompasses narrative, elegy, meditation, an array of voices and selves that tease and subvert. No American poet, as we've had many occasions to say before, has given us more elegant surfaces, more delectable aberrancies, more important and bristling close encounters.

RICHARD HOWARD [2001]

Richard Howard has long been the most subversive of American poets. Often the subversions are sly reversals of an expectation, where a dark prospect suddenly turns promising or is revealed to have been all along sunny. Elsewhere a perfectly scandalous narrative or extended anecdote is told with such obvious relish, with such fondness for the squalid accent or droll detail that we cannot but delight in the awfulness itself. Richard is no respecter of expectations, and often, with a controlled flamboyance just this side of archness, he reveals his appetite for the appalling and the decidedly unlovely. A connoisseur of what one of his characters calls "the wilder dreams," he is never so confiding as when he prepares to spring one of his insidious surprises.

But the subversions and reversals come in many kinds and sizes in Richard's work. Resonant words—'tragedy,' for example, or 'immortal'—are invariably entertained with an alertness poised to spot the hyperbolical or the fatuous in their characteristic employments. Richard is on easy terms with hyperbole or cliché, at least half in love with the occasions they present for playful semantic gamesmanship, or for the insight they provide into our all-too-human folly and pride.

Just so, Richard is an adept of allusion and sublime anecdotage, where the allusion often teases while promising to illuminate, and the anecdote undercuts what it had promised to support. No wonder we find, in Richard, that the word *reveals* is often set alongside or near the word *betrays*, a pair slippery and cunning in their only seeming resemblance.

So, the "categories" of Kant are invoked casually, breezily, without any trace of deep-think, and the biblical Mrs. Lot is summoned simply to underscore the admonition to "look back." As so often in Richard, abundance of invention, superfluity of resource, eccentricities of character and incident, all present to swell a music and enlarge an insight whose final development is blissfully deferred. Richard's imagination is always relentlessly moving on to its next witty piece of wordplay or persiflage. The principle at work here may well come under the heading of "reckless postponements," though never have postponements seemed so prodigal, or recklessness seemed so pointed in its continuous reeling in and playing out of effects.

For many years now I have noted that, in Richard's work, we have satire and encomium, comedy and elegy, the voice of memory and of inflamed desire. The manifold disclosures achieved are, as Richard has himself reminded us, at once ironic and prophetic, and in fact we do not know, much of the time, where the irony begins and the prophecy is wryly or ruefully abandoned. We may say, by way of familiar reassurance, that Richard has long been our master of dramatic monologue, our master of mask and assumed idiom. But this is to say but little, and neglects to mention how far Richard has often strayed from the precinct where he made, long ago, his mark. In eleven books of poetry, to say nothing of the works he has given us as prose writer and translator, he has kept us continuously exercised, thoughtful, amused. Our most genial poet of trespass and of "odd disfigurement," he has taught us the lineaments and the inexhaustible pleasures of avidity.

MARY KINZIE [1991]

That Mary Kinzie is a poet who follows no contemporary fashion is obvious. Surely few of our poets write with so uncompromising a sense of style, so certain a disdain of the trivial and sentimental, so confident a resistance to the easy associative spontaneity much favored in our period. But however much Mary Kinzie goes her own way, so also does her work call to mind the names of other poets. Stanley Moss reads Mary Kinzie and thinks, somehow, of Marianne Moore, Jean Garrigue, William Carlos Williams. To Marjorie Perloff, Kinzie is "an heir of Robert Lowell," her work distinguished by Lowell's fine irony, luminous detail and meticulous attention to craft. My own earliest take on Mary's work invokes the nimble austerities of Louise Bogan, her deliberately wrought elegance, her ability to move toward the heart of an experience without being fully mastered by it.

Such efforts to read Mary Kinzie by the light of other poets are surely inspired by our sense that she works with the full resources of the modern tradition. Her first published poems display a willingness to move from one mode to another, to attack a subject now with a formalist's rigorous demeanour, now with the high romantic's cultivated eye for the rare and exalted. From fairy tale to philosophical conundrum, from Hölderlin to Borges or Thomas Mann's *Doktor Faustus*, Kinzie combs the tradition and makes intricate, difficult poems all her own. Strong on diction, structure, music, these early poems occasionally suggest—without quite embodying—depths of personality. But for all of their power and felicity, they only fitfully forecast the even more emotionally expansive things to come.

This should not suggest that Kinzie has in early middle age become a confessional poet. She continues to write with the high aesthetic purpose of a committed formalist, and she is ever on the look-out for ambiguity, design, emblem. Even where she is most familiar, most personal, one typically approaches her through a scrim of highly wrought images, sharp contrasts, surprising inversions. The language remains an instrument open to every expressive possibility, but also to purely tonal effects of pitch and color. What in a less disciplined poet would sometimes seem excessive, theatrical, self-regarding, in Kinzie seems at once natural and audacious, a flexing of linguistic muscles and a testing of verbal limits.

Recently Mary has brought out two books, one detailing her strange involvement in America's Vietnam tragedy, the other book about family in which the poet's daughter Phoebe figures as dominant character. One can say, as one would not have said eight or ten years ago, that certain subjects bring out in Mary qualities of voice not elsewhere found in her work. One notes that for all of her continuing emphasis on structure and music, she permits the poems to speak with an accent of emotional frankness which at times can seem the most important thing about them—even where one is noting the sophisticated shaping energies at work in the line. There is nothing in Kinzie's early work to prepare us for the rather homely domesticities of a poem like "Little Brown Jug," with its Hardyesque simplicity and only barely threatened air of tranquility.

We read Kinzie's recent poems with no diminution of aesthetic savor or occasional puzzlement, but with a growing sense of the poet's immitigable engagement with an experience that utterly absorbs and moves her. Though we may remark, still, the virtuosity of the end rhymes in a poem like "Sound Waves"—

presages and gauges, obstacle and enigmatical—we are at least as attentive to the poet's obsessively scrupulous, tender observations on infant life. The performative instinct, the instinct to display, is beautifully balanced by the desire to see, to learn, to edify, to feel. Where there is wit, it is in the service of play and of understanding. Where gorgeous pictures are painted, where, as Kinzie writes in "Melisande," "From the casement/ I could hear the thunder like a hiss invade/ The willows near," the worked-up storybook air is at once a slyly knowing feat of prestidigitation and a means of enquiring into the paradoxes of memory. It is, all of it, quite wonderful.

Alfred Corn writes that "it would be a mistake to try to put a limit on what Mary Kinzie may eventually accomplish." But I'd sooner say, simply, that Mary Kinzie now fully belongs in the very small company of poets who have arrived, who matter, who are themselves adding to, creating, the stock of available reality.

WAYNE KOESTENBAUM [2001]

The poetry of Wayne Koestenbaum is a mask of confession, at once confiding and elusive, occasionally rueful but mostly ardent and playful. Though the poet himself has invited, courted, demanded the epithet "bad boy," "bad" as in naughty, irreverent, libertine, he is so genial, and so routinely cheerful, that his brief forays into the penitential seem more like momentary digressions than like excavations of a guilty soul. Alert to the existence of what he calls "drifting secrets" and "feverish pietas," he tends in his poetry to celebration and forward movement. Even when he is looking back he is moving on, evoking, dismantling, remembering so as to go ahead and get on with a life that is largely an experience of pleasure. One has no sense, reading the poetry of Wayne Koestenbaum, of balked possibilities, of fatal reluctances or disabling regrets. Rue itself would seem, for this poet, one of life's guilty pleasures, one of those unfamiliar sensations required to provide a variant savor demanded by a sensibility attuned to many kinds of music.

Of course there is more than one kind of Koestenbaum poem, but this poet's voice is remarkably distinctive, its dips and swoons and characteristic grace notes very much of a piece, even where the look of a poem on the page quite confounds the expectations of its reader. The voice is on easy terms with the sacred and the profane, the lyric utterance and the deflationary downdraft. It is smart, very smart, smart as in sassy and indiscreet, but this poet is smart also as in: conversant with just about everything, high and low, near and far, past and present, unembarrassed about his breezy, witty, more than passing command of the "glockenspiel's solo" and "Doctor Dolittle," "Ida Lupino" and "Ezra Pound." If there is such a thing as too smart, this poet is never, ever too smart, so deftly managed are his recourses and allusions, so charming his subversions of sincerity, his quixotic migrations towards and away from the perverse.

It is easy, and not terribly misleading, to say of this writer that he mostly offers up songs of himself, only so do many other writers, poets especially. What matters in this case is that the self of Wayne Koestenbaum is various, protean, recognizably a particular self with a repertoire of characteristics and eccentric features, but a self given to dissimulations and vagrant ecstasies. Some years ago Richard Howard called him "poetry's youngest vampire," by which description he more than intimated the poet's gift for taking possession of not always willing subjects. Fair enough, with whatever aspects of greed and appetite we care to invest this business of insinuation, infection, and possession. Comfortable with his predilections, the poet concedes, in an essay, that "I like irrelevant juxtapositions," allowing us to understand that, where it is himself the poet mainly sings, nothing is for long irrelevant, every juxtaposition a manifest of the poet's tendencies, with all that hilarious term entails. This is a poet sweet and low down, beauty-worshipper and inveterate prankster, in his drawer, side by side, a nude photo of Sophia Loren and "a miniature torah." The self on display contains, as they say, multitudes, sacrilege and benevolent fancy, the instinct to tease and parody, the equally passionate desire, need, to explore "the stiff sensation around my heart."

Of course Wayne Koestenbaum is, truly, one of the most amusing and rewarding prose writers in the country, author of such deeply original books as *The Queen's Throat* and *Jackie Under*

My Skin. But perhaps I'll get to introduce him some other summer as an essayist. For now, may I close simply by recommending this poet as one of our own authentic American originals.

ROBERT LOWELL [1973]

A funny thing happened on the way from the Albany airport this afternoon. Robert Lowell asked me to describe what would happen this evening at our public interview, and when I set it out for him, he said, simply, no, I can't pretend to be speaking only to you when hundreds of other people will be present watching us. I did my best to persuade him that, in our "public conversation," I'd in effect ask questions on behalf of everyone else in the room, but he didn't at all warm to the convention I described.

As a consequence, Robert Lowell has decided to sit this evening largely with his back to the audience, in semi-profile, facing me for the duration of a conversation that should go for about ninety minutes. After that he'll turn his chair, face the audience and accept further questions for about a half an hour—a concession for which, as for so much else, I am enormously grateful.

By now, of course, it is not at all controversial to say that Robert Lowell is the leading poet of his generation. His work has inspired many essays, a growing number of books, and volumes of intelligent praise from his peers. He is the most widely imitated of American poets, the poet younger contemporaries most hope to learn from. At literary parties—dare I say this?—I have often heard one or another of his more famous poems recited from memory by academics, poets, critics, frequently in the almost perfectly imitated voice of Robert Lowell himself. This is not, perhaps, the age of Lowell, but his work, his outlook, the very inflection of his voice, are very much a part of the literary air we breathe.

For well over a decade Robert Lowell's work has been as-

sociated with the word confessionalism. He is said to be committed to the dredging up of unpleasant experiences and to walking
perpetually on or at "the razor's edge." This is, of course, an inad-
equate account of Lowell's project, but it does say something at
least about the work he did in what some have called his middle
years, which saw the publication of the volumes *Life Studies* and
For the Union Dead.

All of Lowell's work has been marked by the intense
expression of private emotion, and it is likely that most readers
think of him as the poet who wrote, "I hear/ my ill-spirit sob
in each blood cell,/ as if my hand were at its throat." But in fact
Lowell does not invariably wear his heart on his sleeve, and often
the manic, battering urgency of his lines is succeeded by accents
less insistent, by a language of dream and drift and caustic or
plaintive melancholy. There is nothing remotely dispassionate
about Lowell's work, but the tendency to self-laceration and
pathos is formally controlled if never entirely mastered. The
perspective in Lowell's work is typically bleak, the voice damaged,
but one never feels that the pathos is calculated, the ruefulness
measured out. There are surprising, tentative, provisional lifts in
this poetry, moments of near-contentment or hopefulness that
provide some brief, modest "loophole" for the thirsting soul.

At this moment it is impossible to say what precisely are
the most significant and enduring aspects of Lowell's contribution to our poetry. The consensus would seem to be that he has
written several varieties of poems that are permanent additions
to the canon. An anthology of his best works would surely include poems written in each of the last four decades, poems terse
and expansive, of childhood and of marriage, politics and history,
the intimate present and the collective past. He has seemed, for
the most part, a poet characteristically tending to fullness, abun-

dance, though often lines are packed in, compressed, their energies only partially released, held in by an unendurable tension. Lowell would seem never to have willfully suppressed anything, and his rage for truth-telling, like his appetite for extremity, is apparent on every page of his work. Still, the effect of the poems, however great the diversity of their forms and ambitions, is invariably one of concentration and release, a relentless gathering in of impressions and introspections and a corresponding, compensatory expense of spirit, a determined, never quite reckless movement into turmoil and blighted discovery. This movement is evident in "The Quaker Graveyard in Nantucket" as in a much more recent poem like "Waking Early Sunday Morning."

Others have cited and anatomized Lowell's technical innovations, his combination of formal intricacy and conversational immediacy, his deep, alternating, sometimes twinned investment in symbol and in declarative utterance, his lurching movement from violent emotion to stunned devotional tenderness or sheer wide-eyed disorientation. This is a poet who has invested in and dispensed with formal conventions as the spirit of the work has moved him to do. He has not sought a dignified, settled manner or opted for a merely well-made poem or a grave exalted accent. But he has, time after time, made it new and made his reader feel that the working through of his poems—their conception and their composition—has been for him nothing less than a matter of life and death. Of all of our poets, he has long seemed to us the most authentically original and the one with the most important things to say—the poet without whom we simply cannot know fully who we are.

GAIL MAZUR [2001]

"Mazur's is a voice to heed," one very enthusiastic reviewer wrote a few years ago in response to Gail's book, *The Common*. Her writing is "honest," this kindly reviewer informed us, and "generous." She tells good, connected stories, and she is, we are pleased to learn, "perceptive." Very perceptive.

I cite this inoffensive notice, which appeared in a 1995 issue of *The Harvard Review*, because it suggests the kind of response Gail's poetry may all too often generate, a response which emphasizes the generosity and wisdom of her work and ignores more or less entirely the play, the music, the fluencies of manner and idiom. No doubt, Gail herself often invites this sort of thing, emphasizing as she so often does the modest humane thoughtfulness without which we are lost to one another. Inspired by her students at a jam session in one poem, she wants them to have "permission to say whatever they want,/ as long as there's no meanness in it,/ as long as words taste better sweet,/ as long as they're true, as long as they move me." And yes, we say, this is good. This is right, though we do well, as readers of this poem and others by Gail, to remember that even without what she calls "the cool protections of irony," Gail often suggests more than she says, and what moves her is not always, not predictably, fine sentiments. Complicated, we think, when we read Gail's poems. Complicated, her relation to parents, death, students, even —occasionally—niceness. To celebrate Gail's thoughtfulness and honesty may be—sometimes at least—to overlook the range of her achievement as a poet.

To say that a writer is honest can be especially misleading when it suggests that she does not have or need a manner. Gail has, like any fully satisfying poet, a developed and capacious manner. It includes the lack of ostentation others have noted, and the mistrust of eloquence. But the manner allows for seizures of lyricism, and for sudden shifts of tone and mood, so that a solemn visit to a father's grave can shift, with the lines of a compact poem, to the fierce determination signaled in the words, "I'll never lie here. I don't want anyone/ to stand, icy-handed, imagining/ my ruined body." Often in Gail's work, the small incident, the mild anecdote, gives way, moves swiftly into a dark register, so that we wonder at the capacity of the seemingly modest poem to allow for so much.

But this is as yet to say not enough of Gail's manner, not enough, in fact, about the particular achievement we are moved to celebrate in her work. The manner, we have noted, allows for shifts of tone and mood. These shifts, however, are more than manner. When, in a recent poem, Gail looks up at the "Tree of heaven,/ the ailanthus," and notes at once that it is "graceful/ and disparaged," we note not merely the unexpected move from the one gentle word, "graceful," to the other, more heavily charged word, "disparaged." We register, with some alerted disquiet, that with that shift the poem opens onto some as yet obscure prospect of moral inquiry. We note also that what seems casually observed in Gail's work, glanced at, is always prepared to participate in something larger, some inquiry beyond casual observation. In the little poem—really, it is little—early juxtaposing "graceful" and "disparaged" we are struck by the way that Gail soon brings back in to her poem those two oddly paired, increasingly resonant terms, and by the way they fuel a sharp interrogation of our capacities for "sympathy" and "pleasure."

But we are struck, again, and perhaps with greater force, by the poet's incorporation, in so frail a structure, of a contained, brief, but decisive swerve into self-consciousness: "And why would I think of it this minute," the poet asks, when she had seemed, "walking head down/ on the flats," preoccupied only with "the peculiar hermit crabs/ scrabbling away from me, manifest/ hysteria in the pearly August/ day?"

Of course there are other things to note about the swerve into self-conscious self-interrogation, like the sudden rich lift in the language, "the pearly August/ day" gorgeously deposited there in a line that had seemed, if only for a moment, to place its emphasis on a "scrabbling…manifest hysteria." But then that is in the nature of Gail's poetry. It accommodates a great many effects, inconstancies, devices, while seeming mostly measured, head down, constant, largely undistracted. That it is open to so much, that it is in its apparently unassuming way consistently venturesome is at the root of its claim upon us.

All of which is to say, briefly, that Gail steadily enlarges our sense of what poems can do, and does so in a way that enlightens, and gives pleasure, and moves us.

HONOR MOORE [2000]

Honor Moore's first book, *Memoir*, carries a comment from Richard Howard, which notes that her "power of loyalty—to parents, to siblings, to her own body—generates that other power, the power of longing, of desire, and of bestowal." An odd way, it seems to me, to think about an impressive body of work, as deriving somehow from a "power of loyalty."

But Honor's poems do in fact inspire that word, loyalty, however much it is the language of desire that most agitates the surfaces of her work and disturbs the instinct for companionable repose. Honor's is a poetry of candor and recollection, in which particular loved others are persistently summoned, addressed, situations rehearsed, tableaux assembled so that the poet can find, again, what draws her, what has made her who she is. We see her, in these poems, again and again, searching the past, scrutinizing gestures and faces, tracking the trajectories of loss or renewal. "I first remember you in Paris,/ blaze of a smile," she writes at the opening of her title poem. In another, she addresses a "Dearest" with the words, "I have resisted these, my first lines/ in more than a year, waiting for you to pass/ like a mood or a winter, but you persist."

The accent here is characteristically patient, a little wistful, solicitous, but we are not surprised at the gradual rising of something decidedly more disturbing: "Set phrases rise to soothe me," Honor anxiously writes—"This too shall pass" or, later, "Broken hearts are nothing new." The poet's memory stirs her to agitation. Warm recollection gives way to memories too disquieting to be comfortably contained, though there is no instinct to settle old scores or descend to recrimination. The task of consciousness, the management of feeling, the amplitudes of the re-examined life: These are what we want and what we get.

Honor's poetry has none of the sly, sleight-of-hand quality we find in other poets working, like her, with an assured mastery of poetic forms but uneasy with the potential transparency of direct language. She feels no need to cloud the window of her poetry, so as to boast of her sophisticated resistance to realism or illusion. There is in her work enough of theatre and device, metaphor and formal gesture, to satisfy our craving for the beautifully made thing. But Honor is never willing to obscure or distort meaning in the service of form. And we are most grateful, in making our way through her poetry, for the curve of experience it presents, for its refusal to settle for confection or caprice, for its steady lyric kindling of the past and its hopeful, ever hopeful rehearsals of passion or affection.

HOWARD NEMEROV [1985]

When I introduced Howard Nemerov here a few years ago, he thanked me very courteously and then complained—perhaps too strong a word, but still, complained—that I did not somehow appreciate the wit in his poems. Never did, apparently never could. In an essay I had written for the *American Poetry Review* I had given the back of my hand to the short poems especially, the ones consisting more or less entirely of witty aphorism and bitter, sometimes hilarious sarcasm. That was perfectly alright, Howard allowed. I was permitted to deplore those slight ephemeral things, as I chose to regard them. I did, after all, so very much like the more metaphysical or elegiac or anecdotal or contemplative of his poems, that is to say, most of his poems. It was not hard to forgive such a fellow the relatively minor defect in his taste or understanding.

But now I wish to make amends, not by conceding anything or coming around to a view I don't hold, but by saying, simply, that of course I have never disliked aphorism or wit, or wished a short poem were longer when it was obvious that the poet had no desire to open it up, to elaborate or discover what was not within him more or less at the brief instant of the poem's inception and rapid unfolding. Howard's best poems of wit are distinguished precisely by their brevity and by their quick turning of a loaded phrase, their sometimes alarming, unprepared, blunt candor. The rapidity of the thing is more important, obviously, than its depth of reflection. The surprise, the momentary access of pleasure, the glimpse of an insight or a mood or a glittering turn of mind: all of these benefits seem the result of something almost gratuitous, a beguiling though not usually genial brio.

The comic spirit informing such works is not characteristically generous, though it is never unduly satisfied with its own cleverness, and if it issues in works frankly one-dimensional, even the slightest things in this vein are neither shallow nor purely verbal. Howard's wit is often nervy, with just a hint of vulnerability sufficient to allay our suspicion of verbal preening or hauteur.

To say, nonetheless, that one prefers the many other kinds of poems is to say, among other things, that Nemerov has been one of our most various and affecting poets and that his essential gifts go far beyond mere cleverness or a mastery of paradox. He has been, in his best work, open to entanglement and emotion, and though one thinks of him always as a quintessentially lucid poet with a cool and orderly intelligence, he is often vigorously if not dreamily associative. There is nothing remotely casual or careless about Howard's poems. They are elegant, finished, even when most humanly complex and open to unexpected incursions of earnestness or didacticism. Where they are, now and again, literary, they are never merely literary, their textures never unduly thick or dense. Some have said that Howard writes in a plain style, but you need only look at ten or twelve or twenty of his best poems to see that the writing is rarely plain in the way of his more naked contemporaries.

Others have surely noticed that Howard's work betrays an interest in politics and history, in tradition and in language, in fractured intimacies and enduring affections. Often the single sections of a single Nemerov volume will be devoted to a particular preoccupation. In this sense, it is foolish to pretend that in essence a rapt, somber meditation on a piece of music like "Lines and Circularities" will fundamentally resemble a very different sort of poem, half rueful, half satiric, on the vicissitudes of marriage or child-rearing. A Nemerov poem is recognizable in one of several possible ways, but not in one single, unfailingly obvious way. You hear in one poem an insouciant caustic melancholy that is decidedly, unmistakably Nemerov, but in some other one of your favorite Nemerov poems that accent is subdued or absent and you discover instead the rapt, tenderly solicitous flight of a man pursuing something large, a mystery for which he has noted the palpable signs but which continues to stir and confound him to the very roots of his being.

This vulnerability to wonder and mystery does not, much of the time, inhibit or deflect the coruscations of Howard's also characteristic irony. Often he watches himself, rapt or awestruck, a mischievous or derisory half-smile spreading tentatively over his poetic features, so that the instinct to weep or celebrate or wonder is sharply or gradually checked. There is nothing decisive in this process, which reflects unstable moods, contradictory patterns of expectation and disillusion. There is, more than occasionally, a tragic accent in Howard's work, but it is clear that he mistrusts it, mistrusts his own propensity to darkness and melancholia and finitude. The tensions at work in the poems make them at once disconcerting and wonderfully various, poems of defeat and renewal, of scrupulous reflection and an odd, sometimes harsh, compromised exhilaration.

JOHN PECK [1998]

W.B. Yeats wrote, and spoke, of the fascination of what's difficult. Recent much-honored poets, from John Ashbery to Jorie Graham, have often given their devoted readers head-aches, what my hysterical mother used to call conniptions. Even more accessible poets in the years since the advent of high modernism have been pleased to send their readers off to libraries and classical dictionaries and—who knows—patient educational consultants, sometimes called professors—who are paid to re-assure all concerned that the stuff on the page really is, er, difficult, and that it is not our, er, intellectual deficiencies that make it all seem so hard.

The poet and critic Randall Jarrell began his 1953 volume entitled *Poetry and the Age* with a memorable essay called "The Obscurity of the Poet." There, Jarrell concedes that sometimes "the poet seems difficult because he is not read, because the reader is not accustomed to reading his or any other poetry." But that is not a very interesting case to talk about in a room of people who do actually read poems, and like them. More interesting is the fact that poetry, all poetry, is often difficult. The poet and critic Matthew Arnold, as Jarrell reminds us, said "that there was hardly a sentence in *Lear* that he hadn't needed to read two or three times." Of course this condition didn't frustrate Arnold, and in general it is fair to say, with Jarrell, that "people of the past were not repelled by this obscurity" of poetry, and often, in fact, "treasured it," for reasons we need not quite go into just yet. And of course, it is notoriously hard to know, or to say, why one particular difficult poet, say Dylan Thomas, should be so enormously popular with his contemporaries, while another difficult poet, also very accomplished, is not. It is no use declaring that nowadays readers invariably like their poems clear, for clearly this is not so, as several examples will show. But there is little doubt that a difficult poetry which is difficult beyond what needs to be looked up in a dictionary or encyclopedia will seem harsh and forbidding to a great many readers who would otherwise warm to that body of work.

All of this is apropos the work of the poet John Peck, who is with us tonight and who will provide a test case for some of the thoughts we hope to share on the subject of difficulty in poetry. As it happens, the current February issue of *Poetry* magazine contains a very interesting and very favorable review of Peck's work, a review in which the reviewer argues with himself over several pages about what he feels to be the intolerable or excessive obscurity of Peck's poetry. Why, the fellow plaintively asks, does Peck have to be so hard? Why can't he just, well, you know, relax a little, and let the rest of us just sort of lean back and let the melodious accents roll gracefully over us? In the end—and this is a great pleasure to say—our very intelligent reviewer decides that the pain he went through as a reader was more than worth putting up with, and that Peck is a thoroughly satisfying and accomplished poet, one of our most brilliant and original, in fact.

I first published a long poem by John Peck in *Salmagundi* in 1972, and I have been publishing, enjoying and struggling with his poems ever since. Often over the years we have talked with one another, and with Barry Goldensohn and Marc Woodworth, about the obscurity of the poet and the obscurity of Peck's poetry. We have not always seen eye to eye on this topic, or on particular poems inspiring our debates. But tonight we've decided to make the poems of John Peck and discussion of their beauties and difficulties central to a public event. This has been a long time coming, and though we know we can only scratch a few surfaces in the discussion of a vast and complex topic, we also know that everyone present will be moved, ravished even, possibly, briefly, infuriated, by the poems themselves, which John will read to us.

Often, always, difficulty in poetry is a matter of language. John Peck is not a compulsive punster, but he plays, compulsively, with sound patterns and with the forms of words, so that, in a single sentence, the determination to employ the words *came, come to,* and *coming* will potentially make for a teasing and, yes, difficult construction. Sometimes, to suggest speed, as in the mind's rapid flitting about from one subject to another, nouns are lined up sequentially with no separations or caesuras between them to help us keep them distinct. More than occasionally words are chosen for their capacity to suggest something vast or indeterminate, a sensation or an intimation of the never-to-be-encompassed: so, a "destination" is said to be "molecularly here yet moving vastly into announcement." This poet is ever alert to the "unreadable signal" and the variety of "showings-forth" that may leave things dim, impalpable. Objects, sometimes gorgeously, lavishly evoked, are, before long, in the blinking of the poet's eye, glimpsed "smearing into shadow." The poet neither fears nor avoids abstraction, but courts it, summons it, clearly at ease with "human process," "the rupture of abomination," "the incalculable and unmanageable system."

All this, and more, in Peck, makes for difficulty, the responsive, readerly mind routinely taking in more than it feels it can handle, but charmed, exercised, moved by the achieved mastery of the thing, by the yeasty, circuitous and steadily unfolding webs of meaning. This we shall see and learn to love everywhere in Peck's writing—so help me, John Peck.

ROBERT PINSKY [1997]

In a poem called "The Unseen," included in his 1984 volume *History of My Heart*, Robert Pinsky visits a death camp in Krakow. The poem begins slowly, in rain, and it carefully notes in passing "the low brick barracks" and "the heaped-up meticulous/ mountains of shoes, toothbrushes, hair"—what the poet summarizes as "the whole unswallowable/ menu of immensities." The words, there and at other points in the poem, are particularly mouth-filling ("heaped-up meticulous/ mountains"), as though the speaker were accumulating substance to be expended explosively further on. We are not surprised that he should think of "Biblical phrases: I am poured out like water; thine is the day and thine also the night." We are prepared entirely for a dream, in which "I am there; and granted the single power of invisibility, roaming the camp at will," then, "kill kill kill kill, a detailed and strangely/ passionless inward movie: I push the man holding/ the crystals down from the gas chamber roof, bludgeon/ the pet collie of the Commandant's children" and so on, until, addressing the "discredited Lord of Hosts," as Pinsky calls him, the speaker wonders at "the secret" buried perhaps in his "red heart."

The accents of this magnificent poem range all the way from incantation to rage, from the hypothetical to the informational. The speaker blazes with retributive fury while maintaining a tentative distance from his own visionary violence. The "flood of fire and blood" he envisions is tempered by the word "vague," as in "vague flight of fire and blood." The instinct to pay proper tribute even to a "discredited Lord of Hosts" is expressed and held back all at once in a reference to us as "the most/ capable of all your former creatures"—what sadness and anger are conveyed in that word "former"—so that "the most/ capable of all your former creatures" clearly describes those of us who can only stand astonished and trembling at the fact that what happened in the camps was allowed to happen.

Nor does Pinsky allow us any complacent self-righteousness. We who chastise and accuse and shake our heads are sometimes bored and benumbed by what we observe. We ourselves are capable of violence, as Pinsky reminds us. We try to find ways of living with ourselves and accepting somehow that our kind can be human and yet do what is sometimes done.

Of course Robert Pinsky is not a holocaust poet. He has not made of the Shoah his characteristic subject. But in a single poem like "The Unseen" we can observe the operation of a gift and intelligence that are everywhere apparent in Robert's work. We can observe the willingness to take on large themes, as in other works he readily takes on small. We can observe the capacity to invoke biblical contexts and to speak in the accents of prophecy and incantation without any corresponding taint of pretentiousness. We note the movement—assured, so natural as to require no formal transition—between vulnerability and mastery, so that Pinsky can suffer emotion and order it, account for it, in virtually the same breath.

It is, of course, our wish and our habit to say of our best poets, particularly those who have been steadily productive and rewarding, that they get better and better. And of course Robert Pinsky does get better and better, by which we mean that he steadily enlarges his range, takes on prospects he seems not to have embraced before. He writes an elegy built around two lengthy jokes, which he tells in their entirety. He risks a line like "we fowl of a feather we feel we fail" with every sense that a certain kind of alliterative excess or over-the-topness can sometimes evoke emotion like nothing else. Where, in the past, we were usually impressed by what one critic called Robert's "calculated artlessness," we are now sometimes struck by the unabashed theatricality of his writing, his resort to devices and voices. We marvel at Robert's alternation from wit to sentiment, his sense that they need not be held apart.

But we remain convinced, we readers of *The Figured Wheel*, Robert's *New and Collected Poems*, that this poet has never offered us a bad or meretricious poem, that he has—from first to last—invested concrete acts and events with the status of ideas or emblems, and with no diminution of immediacy. He has spoken to us in the perspective of the pagan gods and in comic parodies of overblown lyricism. He has shifted from the casual and the plain-spoken to the more elevated voice of passion or elegy or ambivalent wisdom. There is in Robert's work a capaciousness, a miscellaneous generosity that makes most other poetry seem somehow reluctant. He is now our Poet Laureate, and we are happy to welcome him back.

ROBERT PINSKY [2000]

In a very recent review of Robert Pinsky's latest book, *Jersey Rain*, a reviewer—we won't mention his name—describes Robert's poetry as essentially discursive. No doubt, the reviewer may well have noted in Robert's first book of criticism, published almost twenty-five years ago, that very word, discursive, employed to identify a kind of poetry comfortable with statement and idea and not unduly or compulsively committed to image or sensation. And no doubt, the reviewer might well have observed, in Robert's first books of poems, published, respectively, in 1975 and 1980, that is to say, quite some time ago, a fondness for discursive elements that was apt to seem, at the time, audacious and bracing.

That was, after all, quite some time ago, at the tail end of what was sometimes called The Age of Confessionalism in American poetry, and though the epithet was always more than a little bit misleading, there was never any doubt that Robert's exemplary display of the uses and merits of discursiveness was, well, exemplary and, for many poets and readers, liberating. Rapidly we were reminded of the range of possibility in our poetry, reminded that certain formalist ideas associated with high modernism were in their own way confining, and that the alternative, a kind of primal or nakedly emotional poetry, call it confessional, could also become mechanical and inhibiting. Robert's poems went their own ways, and their ways were unpredictable and various.

But Robert was never, not even in those first books, exclusively a discursive poet. He has sought, in all of his work, to diversify the possibilities and dialects of poetry. And in the many poems and several volumes he has published in the past two decades he has seemed only very infrequently committed to a detached or cerebral stance. The reviewer who can read a long, diverse, complicated and consistently surprising book of collected poems like Robert's *The Figured Wheel* of 1996 or a lyric volume like *Jersey Rain* and come away with an epithet like "essentially discursive" is not a good reader of poems.

This assessment I need not press at this time. Robert, quite obviously, has demonstrated again and again that his poems can do many things. One poem he read here last year interpolates refrain lines from seventeenth century English poetry within a work chiefly dedicated to personal memories of a mother and grandmother, so that the poem is at once anecdotal and elegiac, capacious enough to accommodate gag lines and reflections on myth. In fact, the easy mixing of disparate idioms is central to Robert's procedure. His poems, as we've had reason to note before, typically mix high and low, colloquial and elevated diction, place the "top banana" alongside the "slow dulcimer, gavotte and bow," make the "punchline" and "bric-a-brac" comfortable with a "secret courtesy," allow the formal opening of a poem—"In the beginning was order"—to routinely give way in the very next line to a sequence of "hot cold, dry wet, light dark." It is no wonder that in Pinsky, Ovid is evoked in a contemporary jazz idiom, "playing the changes." Everywhere in this work there are melodious verses and, unmistakable, the enacted instinct for disarrangement and discontinuity: in short, what Robert has called "the unfathomable matrix."

I'll end by stating, simply, that a number of the poems we've heard here for the first time in the last two years—poems like "The Green Piano" and "Samurai Song"—are among our very favorite American poems, worthy to take their place among, along side of, other earlier Pinsky poems, from "Shirt" to "Ginza Samba" and "Poem with Refrains." Just saying the names of those and other Pinsky poems reassures us about the condition of American poetry at the present time.

ROBERT PINSKY [2001]

In an essay in *The Sacred Wood* T.S. Eliot describes, as best he can, the honesty he takes to be an essential feature of genuine poetry. "It is," he writes, "a peculiar honesty, which in a world too frightened to be honest, is peculiarly terrifying. It is an honesty against which the world conspires because it is unpleasant." I quote these sentiments because I happened upon them the other day, not for the first time, and I couldn't help thinking that Robert Pinsky would probably resist them, very much as I do. This is no small thing. Eliot was, I believe, an honest man, or at least an honest poet, one who used poetry to imagine and discover and tell what he took to be the truth. And Robert Pinsky, likewise, seems to me, in that sense precisely, a completely honest poet, never frivolous, never less than a truth-seeker and, with all the ironic self awareness the task often entails, a truth-teller.

But what of Eliot's idea that the genuine poet works "in a world too frightened to be honest" and which therefore finds the poet's work "terrifying"? Pinsky has been writing poems for several decades now, and often he has turned his attention to painful subjects. But he has not written, so far as we can tell, with a sense that his peculiar honesty would seem to the world terrifying. There is, in Robert's work, no sense of an unbridgeable gap between self and other, no pride of alienated majesty to elevate the poet's self-esteem and confirm for him the impossible inadequacy of the little terrified earthlings, that is to say, his readers. His honesty is not, in its essence, an affair of pride at all. It is, rather, a reflection of the poet's conviction that the value we have for ourselves depends upon our willingness, where possible, to call things by their rightful names, to acknowledge and live with

91

unsatisfiable desires, to make and unmake and remake, and never, ever to suppose that there lies, just around the next corner, some final consolation or irrevocable single truth.

Of course it is hard to read Eliot's lines about honesty in poetry and relate them to the varieties of ordinary pleasure Robert's poems rehearse for us. To suppose, with Eliot, that the world "conspires"—that is Eliot's word—conspires against the poet and the honesty he would practice is to be, as a poet, suspicious, potentially bitter. The poet, or persona, who speaks in Robert's work is neither bitter nor, by disposition, suspicious. His is not what is sometimes called an unhappy consciousness, poised always to recoil from the world, which the unhappy consciousness regards as fatally unlovely, disappointing. The honesty of Robert's poems is an expression of his openness to possibility and to hope, of his willingness to believe that things may sometimes turn out to be better than they seem, or that from bitterest despair there may emerge something valuable, if only an enhanced understanding of what it is to be human. Like William Carlos Williams, a poet for whom Robert has an especial fondness, he ranges freely over a wide range of emotions, occasionally taking his own pulse, but mostly attentive to the lives of others and the tumultuous life of the culture in all of its dimensions. There is never in Robert's work anything condescending or impatient, and though he might not quite agree with Williams that, as Randall Jarrell wrote, "The differences between men are less important than their similarities," he is never less than clear-eyed and delicately discerning, as willing to admire where admiration is required as to observe and register what is ugly or indecent.

We would not, surely, say that in Robert there is an " invincible joyousness," but there are in all of Robert's books surprising accessions of "fresh gaiety," "a wonderful largeness" of spirit, a willingness to acknowledge and invite tenderness, and also, no doubt about it, a tough unsentimental candor. Detachment is but one important strategy in Robert's work, wit and humor leavening agents in a poetry that is never ponderous, ever fleet in its motions, but richly musical, resonant, the carefully tuned instrument of a "perfection"—I almost close here with words from a Pinsky poem—a "perfection imagined just before unperfecting/ itself as if by impulse."

In that impulse—to unperfect the imagined perfection, to roughen the surface of a mellifluous line, to tell a joke and fit it exactly to the purposes of elegy, to mix high and low, jazz idiom and elevated diction, homely sentiment and spiritual yearning —in that unperfecting is Robert Pinsky's perfect honesty.

JANE SHORE [2001]

Jane Shore's latest book of poems, *Happy Family*, sports an epigraph from Randall Jarrell's poem, "Thinking of the Lost World." It reads, simply, ". . .All of them are gone/ Except for me; and for me nothing is gone—." No doubt Jane wanted those lines at the front of her book because they formulate, succinctly, a sentiment she shares. And, in fact, the poems collected in Jane's book do embody that sentiment, and do so in a way that occasionally calls to mind the nostalgias of Jarrell, his predilection for looking back even when, as he makes perfectly clear, the past to which he harkens is a country he'd not wish actually to live in again. I hear that note in Jane's wonderful poem, "Happy Family," where a contemporary family dinner at a Chinese restaurant calls to mind the Saturday night take-out Chinese meals of Jane's childhood. "Not all happy families are alike," she quips halfway through the poem, by which time our brief acquaintance with Jane's "somber" mother and "drained," "exhausted" father has instructed us in the appropriate way to read the word "happy." Yet the predominant accent in Jane's poem is by no means dark, and by the time, at poem's end, Jane's present family pries open the fortune cookies containing "our three fates," we know that comedy and joy are at least as much a part of Jane's poetic universe as misgiving and regret.

That this is no small matter need hardly be said. Joy, especially, is suspect in the serious poetry of the last hundred years or so. It is associated, typically, with the unexamined life, with willful blindness and sophomoric fantasy. Oh there is, to be sure, more than a little joy now and again in the poetry of modernism. And there is, more than occasionally, high comedy in some of the poets we continue to read and admire. But Jane's work displays uncommon vulnerability to joy, a hunger to see pain and unfulfillable longing and loss as, in some essential way, potentially comic, each new accession of distress a replay of some earlier distress, and therefore somehow natural, more or less understood, accommodated, not an obstacle to present joy but an occasion to take some pleasure in what, after all, exists and may continue, for some small time at least, to afford us further pleasure.

Though there is, in Jane's work, no note of a pat adult wisdom achieved and settled, there is, in her recent book especially, the accent of what I can only call equable though never complacent acceptance. It is an accent I associate with Jarrell, more than with any other American poet, and of course Jane celebrates that link in *Happy Family*, giving one of her poems, "Next Day," the title of one of Jarrell's most famous dramatic monologues, and allowing herself now and again discreet echoes of images and tropes wittily lifted from Jarrell and made into startlingly original passages and poems. One of the most lacerating items in Jane's book is called "My Mother's Mirror," in which the mother "appraised her face/ as if she were considering/ a damaged antique vase, and weighing/ the severity of its cracks." But set this wonderful poem alongside Jarrell's now half-century-old poem "The Face" and you can see at once how much more forgiving is Jane's poem, how it allows in, at a moment of potential anguish, a projected image of the poet's own eventual, imagined face, "unstable/ flesh stretching like the taffy body/ in the funhouse mirror/ at Palisades amusement Park." Though there is, unmistakably, some fear and dread in Jane's poem, there is as well a certain bemused puzzlement. You can't for a moment imagine the speaker in Jane's poem concluding, like the aging speaker of Jarrell's poem, "It is terrible to be alive." The line would seem, in Jane, excessive, willfully dark, a perverse foreclosure of the life to be lived. There are, we feel, in the works of this poet, always available, though perhaps not immediately discernible, compensations, alternatives, remembered beneficent residuums, and we are grateful to this poetry for allowing itself those uncommon recourses.

Put another way, there is in the poetry of Jane Shore a freshness of outlook, even when the dominant instinct is retrospective. The poems seem a vivid refusal of desolation, though there is no reluctance in them to confront the usual varieties of estrangement and suffering. The mind of this poet, we feel, is incorrigibly responsive and awake. She knows the world to be what it is and she will not be betrayed into avowals, false accents that she does not trust or believe in. Others have praised her transparency and authenticity, and that is fair enough. This is a poet who gives to directness, honesty of emotion and fundamental sanity the good name they deserve.

C.K. WILLIAMS [1999]

C.K. Williams doesn't write pretty poems. With rare exception he abjures the ornamental, the fastidious, the polished phrase, the neat emblematic finish of the master craftsman conscious of his mastery and eager to impress. His is a poetry of struggle and voice, prickly and introspective, worldly and engaged. To read the poems is to feel enlarged, challenged, more than occasionally disturbed, surprised by sudden eruptions of meaning, bewildered by the capacious sympathies and hungers of an imagination that can move so readily from certitude to suspicion, from tenderness to pain, from anecdote to soaring reflection. It is no wonder that other poets marvel at the rage for truthfulness, or truth-telling, or candor, in a body of work that wears not only its emotions but its doubts and reluctances and ideas and convictions very much on its long, battered sleeves.

The manic flutter of the poetry is often its most obvious and strangely beguiling attribute—strange because it is not often that insistent struggle can seem so humanly appealing, so fully an expression of a becoming will to get at the truth of things, to unmask the secrets of the heart, to bring pressure to bear on every least and large particular so as to reveal what should be known. The insistence comes in many forms. There is the repetition of key words or phrases, a sudden recourse to an illuminating, obsessively worked, lavishly exfoliating metaphor, or a compulsive re-tracing of the terrain, with every sense along the way that, no matter how often you correct and start again and press forward, you are likely to want to have another go at the conundrums and anxieties that stir you to wonder and to feel. Even when the poet is confident, coming at last, or at first, to a conclusion—"not

97

suspicion,/ mind, conclusion,/ not a doubt about it, not a hesitation," as he tells us in a brilliant poem called "Signs," the speaker in a Williams poem is ever on the edge of doubt, alert to the fact that a part at least of what he is after will be "hard to track," the more obvious things what you "can just make out," the truths revealed apt to be "forgotten, absolutely," too much for our drifting, doubting minds to hold onto. And so the manic urgency in the poems is a manifest of the poet's perpetual susceptibility to puzzlement, his inability or unwillingness to leave anything alone, his attachment to the interrogative, so that *maybe* and *why* and *but* and *wouldn't it* and *mightn't this* and even *yes. no. yes* constitute an inescapable feature of his rhetoric and his outlook.

To be sure, there are occasional poems in which Williams is not so entirely a voluptuary of anxiety, not so insistently a diver into the wreck as a patient explorer of latency. Some of the poems in his latest book, *Repair*, even look slight, almost neat, shapely on the page, with occasional short lines, though it wouldn't take a lot to adjust the lineage and create at once the impression of amplitude and flux and reversal that seems so central to this poet's work, with its characteristic long lines and dialectical tensions, its proliferating adjectives and retards, its intensifiers and qualifiers. There is room in Williams' work for the odd occasional poem, for the small thing that seems, just for a moment, an exception, but in truth there is in the body of the work, surely as it has evolved over the last twelve or fifteen years, an unmistakable accent that has made the poems seem to us so vital, a part of the way many of us think about ourselves. The accent can accommodate love and grief and pity and nostalgia, but it is not principally derived from the will to express those lively or lugubrious emotions. It is the accent, rather, of thought itself, of thought working through the full range of emotions that call it into being. It is the accent of the mind—call it soul, if you will—arguing with itself, discovering how and why we feel as we do, pressing forward, tumbling back, accumulating memories and conjectures and, when necessary, letting them go, then gathering force again, readying, up for the next foray into the stuff of the common experience, shifting its feet to locate reliable terra firma, learning what to call this thing or that, often disappointed or agitated, almost never still or secure, breathing hard, breathing soft, but coiled always to receive some new burst of information, some refreshment of feeling, some access of bewilderment or insight.

Of course we say of such a poet—we can't deny that we are tempted—that he is a philosopher-poet, a psychologist, that his medium is thought, that his gift is for translating experience into emotion and idea. But this is not a man bent on bringing home hard-won nuggets of analysis or wisdom. His gift is not for system or theory but for journeying out and journeying in, with no prospect of completion. The poems of C.K. Williams are at once relentless and generous, prepared to take us through the next labyrinth, and the next, attuned to portents, attentive to things spiritual and debased, prepared to uncover the worst we can imagine about ourselves, but ever alert to the possibility of atonement, absolution, forgiveness, connection. Best to say of this poet that he is acquainted with the night and strong enough to bring to us, now and again, the morning light. This is a poet who delivers the buried life and the ordinary satisfactions into vivid consciousness.

ADAM ZAGAJEWSKI [2000]

A prelude to an introduction beginning with the obvious: Adam Zagajewski is a Polish poet, whose work we read in translation. Strange to say, though, when his first book, *Tremor*, appeared in English translation about fifteen years ago, many of us were astonished to discover that the poems read as if they had been written originally in English, and we have felt the same about the books that have followed. More, though we find in the poems the sensuous expression of an experience radically different in important respects from ours, including the passing references to Soviet tyranny or ravaged Eastern European lives, we have felt from the first that Adam's was, and is, a world poetry, that it belongs to us as much as it belongs to Polish readers. And in tribute to that sense of Adam's work, many of us think of him simply as a great poet, the way we think of the poets we love, whose background we note without conferring upon it a signal importance.

From the beginning of his career, Adam Zagajewski has been a poet of contrasts. He has sought, in poem after poem, to maintain a fine balance—between darkness and light, past and present, joy and weeping, modesty and insatiability, the quotidian and the infinite. In a recent essay, characteristically opposing to one another apparently irreconcilable contrasts, in this case the shabby and the sublime, he seeks to check "the overwhelming predominance of a low style, tepid, ironic, conversational" by asking whether poetry might not also make a place for "a perception of the world's mysteries, a metaphysical shudder, an astonishment, an illumination, a sense of proximity to what cannot be put into words."

As is often the case with great poets, the best answers to the questions they posit in their prose essays or polemics are likely to be implicit in their own poems. If we read Adam's essay and wonder exactly what a balance of opposing characteristics might entail, we find ourselves enlightened and consoled when we confront the poems themselves. There we find the familiar universe, hot and cold, palpable and plump, but with depths, recesses, pale dreams and possible memories, a whole dim realm of elusive signs that together intimate that there is more to our experience than what we see and what we know.

In one of his famous stories Borges writes that "the metaphysicians of Tlön are not looking for truth, not even an approximation of it; they are after a kind of amazement." This seems to me a suggestive way of thinking about Adam's work, not because he resembles the metaphysicians of Tlön, but because he has thought a great deal about the idea of truth, and approximation, and amazement. You do not read a poem by Adam Zagajewski and lift your eyes from the page to find that a determinate truth has been substantially evoked or hammered into place. When he writes that "now we can believe only in the past," he includes the word *only* to indicate that at present we have no clear access to the truths that seemed real to persons in the past. "In the past," Adam writes, "we had faith in invisible things," though now we have only the memory of that faith, and the "consolation"—that is Adam's word—that we may find a way to those invisible things again, with the assistance, perhaps, of approximations.

And what would those approximations look like, feel like, approximately? In Adam's most recent book, *Mysticism for Beginners*, the approximations surface and decline, but they are always, intermittently, around, like "stains of sunshine/ on a parquet floor" or "Black birds" who "pace the fields, waiting patiently like Spanish widows," or like rare moments when "irony suddenly vanishes," when clear blue skies are not merely cozy and "hospitable," but "uneasy." Approximations, these, of invisible, mostly unsayable things, a prelude or "pale spark" of true things to come, things near enough almost to imagine, as Adam says, "under the elbow of desire."

But what of the amazement sought by those Borgesian metaphysicians earlier invoked? The word suggests more than a preliminary shudder, more than a restless appetite for shimmering approximations. In poetry, genuine amazement typically comes in the form of, or by means of, resonant epiphanies unfolding before us with the force and surprising inevitability of revelation. And that is what we find, again and again, in Adam's work: combinations of words that astonish us and open up visionary prospects previously undreamed of, "sharp and shining moments" swathed, often, in a darkness only partially obscuring or compromising, so that we come to regard as just and inevitable the immediate glide from "the Dark God of cursing" to "the Lighter God who lives in an apple, in bread," the glide from "bitter" to "sweet," from "fatigue" to "fertile dreams." "We exist," Adam writes, "between the elements,/ between fire and sleep," and we see in his poetry the steady effort to capture the rhythms of that alternation, the simultaneous attraction to consolation and foreboding, the sense that we must hold fast to our residence on earth even as we struggle against the shrinkage of our lives to a manageable, compact, mundane dimension.

The amazement we feel in the presence of Adam's work is—strange to say—a steady amazement, administered not by abrupt shocks, but by an accumulation of sensuous apprehensions and daring tropes. The self questing through the poems is ever in search of suitable habitations for unstable desires, bound, as Adam says, to "diffuse itself, diffuse itself" into shifting shapes, but faithful, always faithful to its own essential melancholy, its sensitivity to pain, its own insistent repudiation of "ancient hatreds," of "thwarted Sundays," its impatient alertness to "altitude," song, sudden joy, the incomparable.

FICTION WRITERS

LEE K. ABBOTT [1998]

If there were justice in the world, Lee Abbott's work would be known and read and re-read and talked about by everyone who reads. As things stand, justice is very limited—I don't think I'm alone in noting this—and the stories of Lee Abbott continue to win prizes, to appear in the annual anthologies of the best American fiction, and to entertain those of us with an appetite for, well, brilliant maximalist writing at a time when more minimal fictions seem still—in many quarters—the going flavor. This is not the time or place to pick quarrels with writers of one kind in order to make claims for writers of another, but surely it is legitimate to say that for a long time now Lee has written inimitably rambunctious fictions that present a standing challenge to some prevailing ideas of literary decorum.

It has been noted, by writers as diverse as Andrea Barrett and William Gass, that Lee writes with an "unstoppable energy," that his line has music and sinew and that his long sentences loop and twirl and halt and proceed with an authority that bespeaks an impeccable sense of the way thoughts develop and events connect. "It was a feeling both disheartening and exciting," he tells us in one of those characteristic long sentences, "having to do once more with going as far and as fast as physics and laws respecting human durability allowed, and for an hour, before he called Willie and while he listened to the blizzard beat at his house, he imagined himself as he had been twenty-two months before— unspeakably happy, albeit strung out and bloated, as attractive as spoiled meat."

That final metaphor—"as attractive as spoiled meat" —lands on us with an appealing seductiveness prepared by the sinuous music of the long sentence. Not for Abbott the timid decorum of more sober stylists committed to brief declarative sentences. Nor is there in Abbott a cautious aversion to strong rhythms, or to the alliterative emphasis of *far, fast, physics,* or *before, blizzard, beat.* Abbott writes with an itchy hand ready to pull out every weapon at his disposal, and he seems never to doubt that what he selects will serve.

Nor is there in Abbott any reluctance to shift gears and to build a paragraph here or there out of sharp, short sentences, which are often loaded with the whimsically accumulated detritus of the age. "The ex-boyfriend," he writes in a recent story called "As Fate Would Have It," "The ex-boyfriend should be named Jake—or Slate: a name as contrived as are hats on hyenas—and he should be an actor notorious for off-screen escapades involving sports cars and semi-automatic pistols. Like a billboard for tanning butter, he should be handsome, and mean as a hammer."

Now we're not likely to know what Abbott was thinking of when he dropped in that bit about "hats on hyenas," but it casts a vivid shadow over everything that follows in the paragraph, and as one William Gass once taught us to see, "there's not a trout [Abbott] can't tickle, a fish for which [he] can't contrive a net." Which is to say, Abbott appears in entirely unpredictable and wondrously effective ways. He may provoke, he may tease, but he impresses us as a man possessed, groping, as Bill Gass also once put it, "groping for trouts in a peculiar river." And who wouldn't wish to be there beside Lee Abbott, shifting around the line and pulling up what's there to be hooked?

Lee knows the world and the people who get into his stories. He writes about us all with forgiveness and wit, and he converts the posture of the down-home story-teller to the slightly off-center acrobatics that make his work continuously appealing. No doubt, some of those cited on the dust jacket of his most recent book, *Wet Places At Noon*, are quite right to say that Abbott's work is "subversive and compassionate," that he has something important to tell us about the life we live. But it's surely a mistake to think of Abbott's stories mattering the way earnest moral fictions matter—when they matter at all. Abbott's words, sentences, and paragraphs, episode units and entire stories, have the steadily endearing effect of making the mind blink rapidly, as someone once wrote. He has no interest in thick conceptual systems, but he is fascinated, and expects that we will be too, by the construction of meaning out of language, by the sheer play of the verbal intelligence as it picks its way among the vaporous and substantial materials of our common experience.

LEE K. ABBOTT [2001]

"Interesting guy," we read near the front of a Lee Abbott story, "—about as predictable as flash flooding." The metaphor tickles, amuses, a form of play, though by no means unduly pleased with itself, set as it is in a prose context that is quick with an unending succession of metaphors, witty epithets, abbreviations, teasing obliquities. The very fecundity of verbal invention is a mark not simply of this writer's, well, fecundity, but of his playful relation to the whole idea of literary decorum, his never-diffident defiance of standard conventions regarding surfeit and restraint. Too much of a good thing? Often Lee proceeds as if he never heard of such a stricture, though you know, as you read him, that he's heard of it, alright, and is determined not to give it a moment's pause. Ought we, really, to beware of those glaringly ready-made expressions the freshman writing teachers circle with their red markers and flag as clichés? Never mind, Lee would seem to say. You can have as much fun with those as you can with the speculation about a character's shadowy girlfriend, a speculation that reads, "Maybe a Vegas showgirl, maybe an oak tree with hips."

And so Lee plunders the language, goes, perpetually, as he might wryly say, for broke, in the course of only a few pages committing sentences like "you are no more supposed to get between it and him than you are between hell and high water." Never for a moment do we doubt that Lee knows exactly what he's doing, so that we smile with him, condescend with him to the conventions, root for him to go up to the limit and, occasionally, over the top, applaud this one—the "eyes about as life-affirming as lug nuts" —or that one about the wife "built like Olive Oyl with the go-get-em' personality of a Doberman Pinscher." Nothing, in any sense, correct there, but ceaselessly animated and animating.

Lee is a writer of short stories who has been at it for long enough, over the course of a half-dozen books, to make us take note, if only briefly, of the fact that he hasn't published, ever, a novel. You can think of few other first-rate American story-writers who have been as singularly committed, as apparently untempted by the white flank of the unwritten novel to end all novels. Of course, that thought prompts the reflection that Lee's prose would seem, in the novel, an excess, that the succession of effects would seem more relentless than he would wish, that our readerly pleasure would soon turn to the wish for less, for—dare we say it?—restraint. Which is, I suppose, to say that Lee has stuck with his short-story medium because he knows, truly, what he is meant to do, and has found ways to continue doing it that continue to delight and give us, just barely, pause to give thanks.

No doubt, all of this emphasis—not at all unusual in celebrations of Lee's writing—on his stylistic mastery and extravagance may obscure what also bears noticing. Lee clearly knows well the world and the people who get into his stories. He writes about us all with a relentless drive to note what is preposterous about us, most especially our refinements and our infatuations, our earnest convictions and the enlightenment airs we put on, often with no slightest awareness that we are putting on a thing. In truth, though, Lee is as comfortable writing about cowboys and convicts as about more rarefied types, and his satire is at once biting and compassionate. He is endlessly fascinated, and expects we will be too, by the construction of meaning out of language, and we are, we are: fascinated, lifted up, and again grateful.

RUSSELL BANKS [1998]

This last year has been, or has seemed to some of us, the year of Russell Banks. The massive novel *Cloudsplitter*, based on the life of the abolitionist John Brown, was published to great and often thoughtful acclaim. Two films based on earlier novels, *The Sweet Hereafter* and *Affliction*, were completed, and though *Affliction* has not yet been released, so far as I know, those of us who've seen both films can say that the originals are beautifully served by both of them.

Of course many of us have been following Russell's work for a long time. We remember, some of us, the publication of *Continental Drift* more than ten years ago, our sense that this was one of the essential American novels. We remember Russell's first reading from a largely abandoned draft of *Cloudsplitter*, his announcement here a year later that he'd quit working on that long treacherous novel and instead had turned his attention to a smaller thing called *Rule of the Bone*, from which he read to us that summer, and which rapidly became another essential American novel, routinely linked with *Huckleberry Finn*, and especially savory in Russell's handling of dialect and speech rhythm.

Russell's strengths as a novelist are, have been, obvious. He has known how to paint on broad and narrow canvases. He combines, alternates, vernacular and lyric idiom with enormous aplomb. Compassionate, fearlessly invested in the vulnerabilities of ordinary people, he has also a highly developed historical sense and the probing curiosity of the born adventurer. Writing in the plain language, he is yet sensitive to period inflection and tactful about the recourse to metaphor. Fiercely committed to chronicling the lives of working men and children, the poor and the dispossessed, he is also deeply interested in extraordinary men and women and in ideas.

Cloudsplitter is, quite clearly, a departure for Russell. He has told us that it cost him a lot to write it, and we believe him, though the novel itself has the solidity and inevitability of a national monument. For one thing, the novel covers a lot of ground with a fluency other writers can only envy and learn from. It is narrated by John Brown's son Owen forty years after the bloody events at Harper's Ferry that made the father's name a legend. Perhaps more to the point when trying to get at the difficult achievement of Russell's book, he allows Owen and his father to speak in an idiom bound to sound strange to our ears, a combination of Whitmanesque expansiveness and Old Testament rant. The father slips now and again into what Owen calls "the antique manner," replete with *thees* and *thous*. Adjectival intensifiers abound—the cough of a bear is "gruff," the call of the owl "dour," the cries of the raven "raucous." Little effort is made to rein in the long-winded accents of the narrator, and Owen is mostly unapologetic about his discursiveness and his sometimes tendentious psychologizing. At each wide turn in the narrative we wonder at the grip it has on us, at our tolerance of digression and special pleading, even at our never secure affection for characters whose fanaticism can seem appalling and disfiguring.

We feel, throughout Russell's long and demanding novel, the writer's deep investment in the questions raised by Owen's narrative, but we are never less than impressed by Russell's determination to stand back, to stay out of the way of the unfolding episodes and arguments. He allows his principal characters all the space and time they need to develop their disdain for ostensibly exemplary liberal figures like Emerson and William Lloyd Garrison, men afraid, in Owen's terms, to dirty their starched shirt cuffs, too content to be men of words. Russell doesn't intervene, attempt to settle things for us. He trusts his story to carry us where it should, resists the temptation to place his thumb on the novelistic scale of justice. Few novels of our time, particularly among those so deeply involved in issues that continue to divide and burn, are so finely disciplined in their renunciation of authorial polemic. In this and other ways, *Cloudsplitter* is not only a work of enormous skill but a work of enormous, fully mature intelligence.

RUSSELL BANKS [2001]

There's no air of striving for effect in the writing of Russell Banks, no trace of the stylistic self-infatuation that repels us, or amuses us, in the work of some of his contemporaries. But there is, all the same, an enormous impression of style we feel in Russell's prose, an impression easy to confirm as we read through the work in his latest book, a collected stories entitled *The Angel on the Roof*. Here we find stories so stylistically various as to confirm for us this writer's careful creation of a voice and rhetoric to fit the intention of each of his works.

To be sure, Russell has often been associated with a straight-ahead realism for which the ostensibly appropriate vehicle is a so-called plain style. And, just so, there is in Russell's work a good deal of faithful observation, unpretentious reflection, curt or fragmentary dialogic give and take, deliberate false starts, sudden gusts of humor or sarcasm, unanticipated accessions of sweetness or anger—all very life-like and convincing, all very engaging. We hear what seem to us perfectly overheard voices, beautifully orchestrated utterances at once realistic in the old fashioned sense that we can easily believe someone would say them just that way and also, at the same time, made-up—as in a little exchange that goes: "Don't let him bother you." "He doesn't bother me. That damn wood bothers me. That's what bothers me."

Plain-talk, that, but encompassed by a style that makes the rhetoric impressive, purposeful, the repetition of the word *bother*, like so much else in Russell, not merely serviceable, right for the speaker and the occasion, but stylish, literary—in the best sense literary.

But listen, for a very different rhetoric, to this, from a story called "Firewood," where a guy named Nelson is taking at 6 AM his first drink of the day: "A deliberate, slow act, as measured and radiant as a sacrament, as sweet to him as the sun rising over the winter-burnt New Hampshire hills, as clean as new frost... thinking only about the vodka as it fits like a tiny, pellucid pouch in his mouth... enters his blood and then his heart and brain, enlarging him and bringing him reheated life, filling the stony, cold man with light and feeling and sentiment, blessing him with exact nostalgia for the very seconds of his life as they pass, which in this man is as close to love as he has been able to come for years."

This passage is, no doubt about it, touched by a frank, expansive, robust, poeticism, where the poetry is a manifest of the writer's effort to confer upon a small man a more than generous elevation. What Russell calls "an exact nostalgia" is in this case a nostalgia for the moments when, confronted by such a person, however limited or awful, it may be possible to embrace him, to imagine him—even this small man—somehow blessed, however provisionally: enlarged. Other writers in the school of realist writing to which Russell belongs might well eschew the unironic use of words like *blessed* and *sacrament*, the heightening rhetoric of "measured and radiant," the intensity-building sequence of "light and feeling and sentiment." But Russell has consistently refused to deny himself the full expressive resources of language. He has gone where he wished to go, and he has used the language with the kind of freedom and conviction that can belong to a writer who knows what he wishes to say and believes—really believes, as in this case he should—in the adequacy of the expressive equipment at his disposal.

Of course there is more to say about Russell, beyond the point that he is a masterful stylist, an adventurous and unpredictable writer. On other occasions here we've had opportunities to savor his command of situations, his capacity to bring to life the past, his communicated feeling for a wide range of people, his willingness to confer upon the fatally weak or injured or provincial the full measure of his sympathy and understanding, his grasp of consciousness in its harsh waywardness. We have even had opportunities to appreciate Russell's wit—who among us present in this auditorium in previous years will ever forget Russell's first reading from *Rule of the Bone*, or the reading of a story called "Cow-Cow"? For the wit and humor of these works we are grateful, and grateful again for what our friend Mr. Ondaatje rightly calls Russell's "tough affection" and "uncompromising moral voice." "I trust his portrait of America more than any other," Michael has written, "—the burden of it, the need of it, the hell of it."

ANDREA BARRETT [1998]

I first heard the name of Andrea Barrett several years ago in a telephone conversation with Nick Delbanco. The real thing, he told me. And there was no telling how far she'd go with gifts that were clearly prodigious. More recently, Nick and I have agreed that there was nothing inflated about his early estimate. To work with such a writer at an early stage of her progress, as Nick did with Andrea, is surely one of the great satisfactions of the teacher's life, and I'm especially glad that we can all be here together to gloat over Nick's judgment and—not incidentally—Andrea's recent achievements.

Of course it was Andrea's National Book Award-winning collection of stories, *Ship Fever*, that persuaded most of us to accept what Nick had already observed. The earlier novels were intricately plotted, richly eventful and lavishly colored, the work of a writer clearly about to emerge as a distinctive presence. *The Middle Kingdom*, though Andrea's third novel, was the first I read, and it seemed to me furiously absorbing, shifting about relentlessly from one setting to another—from the Tiananmen square uprising to the ivy confines of a college campus, from childhood to marriage and infidelity. Flashbacks and flash-forwards are employed with the easy confidence of a writer who knows precisely where she is headed but means to back and fill and anticipate and strategically postpone until every particular has been moved into its most desirable position. For all the sense Andrea's novel conveys of accumulation and steady, patient development, events often succeed one another in rapid succession, so that there is throughout an impression of teeming possibility, prodigal invention, the kind of momentum that allows us to feel how closely disparate events may be linked, consequence follow hard upon consequence, as if things were ordered according to some fatal design.

Ship Fever is, of course, a more miscellaneous volume than any of the novels. The works are told from different perspectives, with about half the stories set in the past, the title novella during the period of the Irish famine, another in the eighteenth century. Figures from the history of science emerge, sometimes even take control of a work. Gregor Mendel vies for attention with Carol Linnaeus, the Swedish botanist whose name is associated with the classification of plants. Contemporary biologist-characters draw us into scientific or medical procedures, but take us ultimately to the unfathomable reaches of human desire and interaction.

Ship Fever is a volume of such utter confidence that it seems at once the sort of thing Andrea has been at for a very long time. The poise is obvious at every turn, never more than in the masterful way that Andrea builds metaphors out of the activities of her scientists. And there is unmistakable confidence in Andrea's willingness to write about the vicissitudes of intellectual women without contriving to make their pursuits seem hopeless or merely an occasion for protest. Reading Andrea's most recent fiction, we feel that we are in the hands of a fully mature and ambitious writer, eyes trained now on the experience of love, now on the demand to understand our human place in the natural world.

That demand is central as well to a new work of Andrea's set to appear this fall and entitled "Servants of the Map." It is a work largely structured around interpolated letters which chart the constancy of affection and, at the same time, the metamorphosis of two people in a relationship marked by long, dire separation. Equally important in this novella-length work is the incorporation of fragments that the husband in the correspondence would like to write, but resists, as well as his careful "editorial" consideration of language actually employed to communicate with his wife. So deft is Andrea's handling of this correspondence and of the intricate narrative in which it is set that we fully realize only at the end how much we have learned—an odd word for our experience of a novella, but still, learned—not only about the people involved in the core relationship but about the passion to know, to investigate, to risk everything that is stable and dear in the pursuit of an understanding that is the ever-beckoning object of scientists out in the far field. No other writer has so lavishly and delicately evoked that passion and made it seem so entirely an aspect of our humanity.

And therefore we are, all of us, eager for the next book, and the next, of this self-described "literary writer" who has found the broad literary audience she deserves.

ANN BEATTIE [1998]

Two years ago, Ann Beattie showed up here with the manuscript of a novella called "Park City," which now turns out to be the title work of her latest book, a massive *New and Selected Stories*. At first Ann worried that "Park City" would be too long for a reading, but it was hot off her word processor, she was eager to try it out, and all of us were rapt throughout the long and memorable reading of that work.

"Park City" had, first of all, a wide range of signature Beattie details, from Tower Records to Orangina, from Catherine Deneuve "looking classy and scintillating" to a father with "a Clint Eastwood squint." The decor of a room interior featured an orange leather sofa that looked "like furniture recovering from a chemical peel." The cuisine of choice included "I can't believe it's not butter spray." Not surprisingly—Ann Beattie has taught us to expect perfect pitch and organization in her fiction—the bits and pieces of allusion and vagrant detail are impeccably well orchestrated. The narrative line courses with a strong forward momentum while accommodating easily all the different kinds of verbal and associative traffic it must carry.

Of course Ann has most often been described in terms that stress her hipness, her mastery of the American scene, her knowingness about the lives we lead and the sometimes delusional stories we tell ourselves. Ann's early *New Yorker* stories, some of the best of them now republished in the *Park City* volume, did in fact capture like no other body of work the face of many people in her 70's generation. Many of those people were unhappy or adrift, empty or disconnected from love or from vocation. Most of them were, more than a little, unappealing, and Ann's readers admired not them but her understanding of them, not what she made of them—she didn't try to make more of them than they desired for themselves—but her cool attentiveness.

Ann's touch was, and has remained, light, and her ability to penetrate surfaces while keeping her distance was never less than admirable. When she poses questions, say, about loving, or betrayal, or dependence, she does so in the sure confidence that just so much of the question will be answerable as is necessary for us to feel that trying to get it in focus matters. Never do we feel that we've been given too much, that what is essentially mysterious, if often commonplace, has been explained away. "He is impossible," a young woman says of her lover in the story "Secrets and Surprises," and "as immature as his friend. Why have I agreed to let him live in my house until he leaves for Denmark?" There is no need, we feel, to rise to the challenge contained in that plaintive question. We need only look back at the opening line of the preceding paragraph—"My lover sits beside me on the piano bench. We are both naked."—to feel that Ann has provided, throughout her story, in many deft glimpses, all that we require to think through the dilemmas of these people at this young stage in their lives.

More than one critic of the late-century fiction scene has complained of the absence of "social fabric" and "big-picture" realism in the work of writers like Ann and Raymond Carver. Such critics demand, in place of detail and shard, wholeness and conceptual system. And, of course, there is a fiction that aspires to a vision of politics and a critique of cultural institutions. But Ann has given us, with a conviction and fidelity that are continuously impressive, an unrelentingly incisive portrayal of the contemporary social fabric. And she has, at the same time, provided something else. She has produced what may well be termed a late twentieth century comedy of manners, in which many of us stand revealed more sharply than we would wish. She has shown us, often at our worst, in our pettiness and dullness of spirit, and she has asked, with wit and with a never gratuitous severity, why it is so hard for many of us to rise to the challenges of life. For all Ann's undeserved reputation as an apologist for the spiritually empty persons she sometimes portrays, there is nothing easy or indifferent in the way she raises hard questions and forces her characters to confront them. Her best work—and there is a lot of it—goes at the important issues with genuine intensity, and offers us something we've discovered we just can't do without.

ANN BEATTIE [2001]

"Of course, anyone would take her for a tourist," a character thinks in a recent story by Ann Beattie, and of course we know precisely where the thought comes from, having learned, in the course of a brief paragraph, that this tourist in Italy is wearing an outfit that unmistakably gives her away: sweatpants, pullover, running shoes. As always in the fiction of Ann Beattie, whole inventories of telling detail are spooled out before us with a relentless, yet casual, unmistakable rhythm. The observing, accumulating, recording eye is preternaturally alert, ever on the lookout for signs, though Ann is in no particular hurry to erect large symbols or to set in place some strict interpretive logic. The looking itself counts for a great deal here, and the signs are more apt to gesture at small things, vagrant impressions, than at permanent insights. Things connect in Ann's fiction, but the author is generally reluctant to insist. We see what she wants us to see, and are invited to follow out the patterns only so far as the particulars do really seem to us to warrant. There is never any danger in a work by Ann Beattie that the signs will mean too much.

No doubt Ann is still associated with words like *minimalist* and *laconic*; her characteristic take on things is said to be smart and ironic and detached. And, to be sure, there is much even in Ann's recent work to support this sense of her. In a story called "The Siamese Twins Go Snorkeling," the color of a plant is "as purple as Liz Taylor's eyeshadow in the sixties," a simile at once improbable and playful, which creates, between author and reader, a bond of complicit smartness and ironic wit. Yes, we say, we know that this is arch, that this is a way of describing something and of having a good time, and at no one's expense in

124

particular. Just so, when, on the next page, the reference is to "A little Leonard Cohen from the CD player," we are not at all put off by what follows, namely: "Cohen nouveau—a treat that arrived with the springtime, exported par avion by his friend Goldman, to be enjoyed quickly. Much better than Leonard Cohen's old shit. The future? Cohen's voice rattling along like tires riding over singing gravel." The pleasure we take in this has much to do with our complicated reception of the several key markers, each of which plays us as only Ann knows how to do. The expression "Cohen nouveau," for example, and "exported par avion" are delectable little teasers pointing playfully without meaning anything momentous. At one level they embody the sort of fake sophistication that a drop into French in a casual discourse would once have signaled. They have, in other words, the look of satire, where the target of the satire would be the sort of silly and pretentious person who would actually use such expressions.

But Ann's writing, here and elsewhere, is at some remove from that sort of satire, so that the terms "Cohen nouveau" and "exported par avion" are lighter, more playful, more generous, signaling the wit of the person who uses or thinks in such terms while knowing how silly they are and therefore how entirely the resort to them makes us superior to those who would avoid them. There is in this a sort of implicit one-upsmanship, and it is their fondness for that sort of reflection that makes many of Ann's characters wryly amusing, to themselves and to us.

We might note, too, in the passage quoted, the quick, surefooted metaphor, " Cohen's voice rattling along like tires riding over singing gravel." How often in the past has it been said that Ann has not much use for metaphor, that her writing is spare and unadorned? But there is, in fact, in Ann's fiction, a growing recourse to the coloring and intensification that metaphor often enables, and there is a growing pleasure, too, for the reader trained by Ann's prose to expect the unadorned and frequently, therefore, surprised by the little surges of unselfconscious metaphor and texture.

Everyone at a writer's institute knows that Ann Beattie has long been celebrated, more than occasionally envied, and sometimes chastised as the most acute chronicler of what one reviewer called "the lifestyles of the narcissistic and disconnected." Every one of her readers surely registers the "uncanny air of the actual" in her novels and stories, the frequently dead-pan, right-on wit. But only in the last few years, since the publication of her new selected stories volume, *Park City*, have literary people really caught up with the enormous expansion of Ann's range, her growing interest in characters one would not have thought quite worth the investment before, her accessions of tenderness, her—dare we use the word here?—her sympathetic concern for the fate of her characters, her willingness occasionally to let the temperature of her prose rise to the point where it can risk elegy and mournfulness. Yes, even now, it is true, as Margaret Atwood wrote, "a new Beattie is almost like a fresh bulletin from the front." But Ann's work is by no means to be confused with an ephemeral snapshot or a strident news-flash. With sometimes punishing acuity Ann permits us to see large, one is tempted to say permanent, aspects of our common, contemporary reality, and her poise, sense of timing and nose for the phony and ridiculous provide the constant pleasure that only genuine literary art can provide.

SAUL BELLOW [1995]

Saul Bellow last visited Skidmore College twenty-one years ago, and those of us who were around at the time remember his visit with enormous gratitude and pleasure. He was more than a little embattled in those days, a participant and a target in the culture wars of the 1960's and 70's, quite as he has remained in recent years. But for all the sound and fury generated by his participation in these culture wars, he has seemed to most writers and literary people simply the best American writer in the second half of this century. Many a New York intellectual has said—often with a combination of pathos and wistfulness—that Bellow has written the novels they would have written, if only they had been smart enough, or written better sentences, or known enough about the world. Some of us, less inclined to wistfulness or envy, have felt that Bellow has written the great and necessary books for Americans of his generation and ours, and that it is a privilege to be so represented.

Of course a great many books and essays have been devoted to the writing of Saul Bellow, and many in this audience have read the novels for themselves and discussed them in classes. But it may be well, very briefly, to remind ourselves that Bellow has been not only the most satisfying of our writers, but the most venturesome. His novels range from melancholy realism to intellectual fantasia, from moral fable to picaresque ramble, from comedy of manners to literary satire. His gifts have included an extraordinary capacity to animate ideas and a capacity for sheer spectacle. Characters are drawn sometimes with the tenderest affection, sometimes with pure venom. The focus shifts wildly from sexual derring-do to transcendental mysticism, from the decline of the west to the decline of male potency. The tough-spirited and the ineffectual are so ceaselessly juxtaposed that it is not always easy to tell them apart. Best of all, the language, the wit, the forward momentum of the thought, the frequently neurotic inflammations of desire, the obsessiveness about redemption and transcendence—all conspire to produce a vitality, a tension, an abundance utterly unique in literature.

Next spring, *Salmagundi* magazine will devote to Saul Bellow a special feature, with contributions by several leading writers. A transcript of the interview that you are about to witness will be the centerpiece of that issue. Contributors will say, in their various ways, things that we have heard before, and, occasionally, things that are new. Some will tell us that as writers they were chiefly impressed by the "life-force" within Bellow's language, its irrepressible "prodigality." Others will share their surprise at the irrepressible "yea-saying" that "roars…like a lion" from a vision that is essentially dark. Still others will linger over "the glamour of thought" in Bellow and his peculiar, persistent skepticism about that very glamour and about the high modernist investment in ideas. "They don't get us anywhere; our speculations are like a stationary bicycle," one of Bellow's characters complains, in a way that seems at once characteristically hilarious, earnest and perverse to more than one of Bellow's commentators.

Of course there is more, much more, to say of Saul Bellow, and of the reflections—contrary or devout—he has long inspired, reflections that often focus, with wonder, on Bellow's insistent gift for doing the very thing every first-rate writer would wish with all his heart to do. "Whereof we cannot speak, he speaks": so writes Leonard Michaels of the writer who, above all others, embodies for him, as for so many of us, *sprezzatura*, who speaks, over and again, "to your eyes, ears, and kishkes."

Please welcome the creator of Augie March, Henderson the Rain King, Moses Herzog, Artur Sammler, Tommy Wilhelm, Charlie Citrine and ever so many others who have won a permanent place in our literature.

ELIZABETH BENEDICT [1998]

Elizabeth Benedict's most recent book is—shall we call it a manual?—entitled *The Joy of Writing Sex*, and though it is obviously not a work of fiction, it conveys several qualities of mind we discover in Liz's novels. "Losing one's virginity," she writes at one point, "has more in common with getting a driver's license than we like to think. The plastic-sealed card that fits in your wallet doesn't mean you know all you need to know about driving; it means you've been given permission to find out firsthand everything you don't know." A compact and pretty formulation, don't you think? Never mind that losing one's virginity actually has very little in common with getting a driver's license. The comparison is a piece of wit, and it opens up considerations we might not otherwise wish to entertain. More, it is provocative without being tendentious. We know there is a sense in which Liz is asking us to take seriously this bit of speculation, but we can also hear in her voice the pleasure she takes in a trope that has mostly its cleverness and freshness to commend it.

Liz's delicious manual includes excerpts from the work of writers she admires—Joyce Oates, Iris Murdoch, Edmund White—and reflections on writing sex by writers like John Updike, who wrote to Liz that "writing my sex scenes physically excites me, as it should. I don't enjoy other writers' as much as my own." Reading Liz's sex scenes, especially in her third novel, *Safe Conduct*, we are apt to believe that she is, as it were, at one with the redoubtable Mr. Updike, on this one score at least. And though Liz builds up around her sex scenes so much emotional texture and psychological freight that physical excitement may not be quite so central to our experience of them, we are surely

130

stirred, and moved especially by what the sex reveals about Liz's characters.

Liz is, in fact, most aptly describable as a writer for whom character is of primary importance. She is interested, clearly, in a great many things, and even handles political intrigue with an appealing confidence, never permitting political ideas as such to get in the way of the ongoing narrative design. But her skill is most impressive when she is developing character, registering the shocks of feeling and suspicion that are so much a part of complex relationships among mature, worldly people. Though it is often the case in Liz's fiction that characters mistrust relationship and think of their bonds as entirely provisional, there is always the prospect that life itself will confound their expectations. Subscribing, as characters in the novel *Slow Dancing* do, to "a 21-day rule about relationships," they nonetheless find themselves embroiled in long-term affairs that confuse and even disturb them. Seasoned veterans of sex wars and other more far-flung campaigns, adept at concluding—as one character has it— "that sleeping with men you didn't care about was an acquired taste and that she had acquired it," Liz's characters may nonetheless surprise us, and themselves—like the documentary film-maker in *Safe Conduct*, who marries an older man who has lost his son because she is moved by the openness of his grieving.

Liz's characters generally know how to have a good time, and their author knows how, in pursuing them, to raise questions about the life we lead, while permitting us to remain stimulated and amused. But there is also in Liz's fiction a remarkable alertness to the pain that is never very far from the surface of a happy life, and a clear-eyed sense that our wit and nimbleness and light-footedness will never be enough to protect us from what is out there. "What do I know and what do I invent?" one of Liz's characters asks, and though the question remains in some sense open, we understand that in Liz's universe we do not invent or control most of what is essential in our lives.

CLARK BLAISE [1999]

Read any page of a novel or memoir or story by Clark Blaise and you know at once that you are in the presence of a writer of singular brightness. The effects range from the visceral to the cerebral, from the wildly comic to the plangent and melancholic. Everywhere there are sentences, phrases you want to write down, to hold onto, to appropriate. Characters often speak and think in splendidly witty and articulate sentences. A woman reflects on aging as "the pendulous tristesse of breasts." Another characterizes the males of her acquaintance as "competent, agile, undemanding." A settee drawer is a "little sarcophagus of wine glasses." An assemblage of mixed-breed dogs is observed as "heroic and unfortunate, the abject, sexually excited tail-wagging, the foamy-jawed growling, the ferocious timidity of a confused enthusiasm." The reader proceeds from page to page with ever growing pleasure and the excitement you feel in the presence of a writer who makes every sentence count. When Clark invokes, in the opening lines of a story, equations and parabolas and coordinates, you know that he isn't indulging in finger exercises but setting up figures he intends to work and elaborate over the developing course of his fiction.

Though Clark was born in North Dakota, grew up mostly in the deep South, and went to school at Harvard and the University of Iowa, he is descended from Canadian parents, spent a good many formative years of his life in Canada, and is often regarded as a Canadian writer. The uncertainty about his true place has led him to write often about unhousement, marginality, estrangement, and he has raised questions about cultural difference to the level of myth, where they operate with peculiar force.

Though Clark's work seems usually to be focused on himself, one never senses in his work a narrow self-absorption. When he goes out, in fiction or memoir, in search of his own lost father he writes as if lost fathers were at the center of the common experience. Just so, though cultural difference, particularly as between Canadians and Americans, may seem of little compelling importance to most of those living south of that extensive borderline, Clark invests in the exploration of that difference such reserves of emotion that it comes to loom large for his readers as well.

In fact, Clark's handling of crises and events, large and small, is such as to make of every eccentric particular, as of every seismic shifting of the cultural ground in his fiction, compelling aspects of inescapable human conditions, so that adolescent sexuality circa 1952 becomes in Clark's story "Identity" a gateway to knowledge about parents and children, repression and sublimation, cruelty and the death instinct. Darkness is represented in ways that are at once frightening and wildly comic, bizarre and entirely believable. A mother-son relationship is observed by an adolescent boy with an excitement and confusion that are viscerally affecting and in every sense stimulating to us as readers. "They had the cheaper, one bedroom model," Clark writes, "but every time I entered it I was struck by the fumes of something lurid. Peter's mother wasn't much older than thirty, her hair was black and ringletted, her body lean and firm, her habits loose and leering. She'd strung clotheslines across the living room and her entire stock of lingerie and negligees was usually on display ... There wasn't a time I visited when his mother was up and moving that I did not come out of that apartment with something shocking to me, some hunk of flesh observed or knowledge that would stimulate me like some laboratory rat in an uncontrolled experiment."

As always in Clark's work, the writing here is sure, the control of pitch impeccable, the flourishes of language purposeful and delectable, the eruption of metaphor at once audacious and natural. An entire world emerges in cunningly selected details, characters in deftly glimpsed physical particulars, odd gestures, speech fragments. Theoretic categories—the Oedipus complex, infantile fixations—are summoned and tried out with the sense that experience is mysterious enough to warrant our recourse to anything we can get our hands on, so long as we don't allow the categories and explanatory principles to do our thinking and feeling for us. In Clark's hands we feel that everything is at least a little strange and more than a bit familiar, that there is nothing without intrinsic interest, and that Clark is always prepared, poised, to discover it for us.

In short, whether he is writing about displaced central European intellectuals or American continental drifters, about guilt or the family romance, Clark has fashioned works of extraordinary beauty and virtuosity. For twenty years he has been one of my favorite writers, and it remains one of my great pleasures to introduce him.

CLARK BLAISE [2001]

A month or so ago I wrote an introduction to a volume of stories by Clark Blaise, soon to be published in a collected four volume edition of Clark's shorter fiction. Reading through the works assembled for this forthcoming volume, a number of them familiar to me from readings in this very room, I was struck, not for the first time, by the extraordinary drive of Clark's work, the continuous agitation of surface, the communicated impression of verbal discovery and gradually unfolding cognitive awareness. Clark is a restless, searching writer who is as compelling at the sentence level as at the levels of paragraph, page and finished work. Even the mundane assumes, in Clark's writing, the quality of the slightly off-center, the language itself so brisk with invention that nothing can seem altogether stable; the material world in the stories is palpable, there, but subject to the plausible deformation that a rich novelistic language can accomplish. There is nothing fussy or artificial about Clark's writing, but neither is there any sense of that reserve, that discreet concern with a merely formal elegance that would be inimical to the spirit of this fiction.

More than fifteen years ago, in his book *Resident Alien*, Clark promised his reader "a journey into my obsessions with self and place," obsessions in good measure deriving from the facts of a life part American, part Canadian, part Third World resident alien, part greedy, voracious inheritor of European cultural benchmarks and appetites. Those obsessions are everywhere present in Clark's work, in his novels and stories as much as in his travel-writing and memoirs. They are, without question, at the center of fictions set in the American south as they are central to those set in Pittsburgh or mittel Europa. Whether coming-of-age narratives or love stories or tales of balked ambition, Clark's work has about it an air of strangely vivid, never grim disenchantment, as if the writer were so amazed at the accumulating shocks and reversals of his experience that he could never find it less than provocative, amusing, ample material for a lifetime's speculation and creative reconstruction. The uncertainties of place and identity that are evoked with sometimes savage candor are discernable throughout, so that we feel, as we move from one of Clark's books to another, the familiar, ever renewable set of obsessions.

For all the turmoil in Clark's work, for all of his tendency to see in the special anguish he studies the marks of a more general condition, there is no trace of a merely theoretical anguish, no deliberately portentous assembling of darkly telling anecdotes to confirm the resolutely downward drift of a settled disposition. Clark's facts and metaphors proliferate like washes of color saturating a canvas that has been carefully primed to absorb them, but much of the color is significant for the mood it imparts rather than for any point it may be said to underline. The images in Clark's fiction often carry a powerful charge, but they are with rare exception "passing, irretrievable." Even where there is a smell of death or apocalypse in the air, the imagery and the tenor of the writing mostly bespeak a gradual decline, what Clark calls a "long disenchantment." There are no grand disclosures in Clark's work, though there are small, stinging shocks, and the language, for all its occasional bluntness, gathers its effects patiently, with a special feeling for the lures and deceptions that make any prospect of disclosure seem both appealing and improbable.

There is much more to say, but I'll end by recommending, simply, Clark's latest work, a delectable work of nonfiction entitled *Time-Lord*, which combines history, biography, cultural criticism and literary anecdotage.

J.M. COETZEE [1992]

In the novel *Waiting for the Barbarians*, J.M. Coetzee writes—as he has himself acknowledged—"about the impact of the torture chamber on the life of a man of conscience." Other writers have also taken up this subject, not always with the same objectives but with a considerable effectiveness. What distinguishes Coetzee's novel from the others is not a theme or an angle of vision but something I can only call an underlying moral sentiment. This sentiment we recognize the moment we consider what Coetzee might have done in depicting torture. Though he dramatizes the situation of torture and uses a novelist's language to evoke suffering, he never quite gives himself to a full depiction of physical brutality. Understanding—so we feel—that the torture chamber may have for us a strange, perverse fascination, he refuses to give in to anything like a pornographically arousing depiction, to allow us to revel in cruelty or pain. While insisting that we look hard at the obscenities practised in the name of the state, or the law, he resists any recourse to familiar clichés or grand metaphysical noises. The sufferings evoked are on a consistently human scale, and the evil practised by Coetzee's characters calls to mind nothing satanic or unduly exotic. Neither is there any indulgence of uplifting moral sentiments, false heroics or chic theories focused on the oh so fascinating connection between violence and the sacred. As in his handling of other issues, Coetzee's treatment of torture is at once restrained and vivid, immediate and enigmatic, sober and impassioned. Not for Coetzee the glib speech-making, posturing and position-taking that typically compromise the work of novelists with all too palpable designs upon us.

Coetzee has been described as a realist, but in all of his fiction we are aware of something that stands between us and the material of the narrative. The critic Denis Donoghue once spoke of "a certain haze between the events and their local reference, a suggestion of ancestral lore and balladry." That is exactly right for particular sections even of so apparently straightforward a work as Coetzee's *Life and Times of Michael K*. In *Waiting for the Barbarians* the "something" out there to which we respond along with the action is an aura of allegorical control, the sense we have that we are to work at deciphering things otherwise obscure or misleadingly accessible to our intelligence.

But readers of Coetzee are most especially claimed by an attention to language that makes it difficult indeed to suppose that there is but one way to read the novels. In *Waiting for the Barbarians* we consider the effects of the administrative language of oppression. The novels *Foe* and *In The Heart of the Country* are no less dextrous in their very different reflections on language, the one probing the relation between writing and speech, voice and silence, the other ruminating obsessively on what it calls "idiot dialogues," the corrupt "language of hierarchy," the failure to find a language of the heart.

Of course, in all the attention paid to language and politics in Coetzee, the obvious is sometimes overlooked. No one in our time writes a better English sentence, brings so much to life in so brief a compass, and manages so well to combine lucidity and implication. It is tempting to praise Coetzee chiefly as the author of works that bear witness to the tragedy and trial of his people, but it is well also to think of him as an explorer of the inner life and a true poet of consciousness. To be sure, one typically comes away from Coetzee's books filled with grief and shame over what human beings do to one another, but it is not South Africa alone that inspires those emotions, and not those emotions alone that grip us. One feels, quite as urgently, a sense of wonder, of gratitude, for all that language can do to make thinkable the unthinkable. That is what the greatest art has done in the past, and that is what we have come to expect from the work of our guest.

J.M. COETZEE [1996]

Novelist, political thinker, cultural critic, linguist, theorist, anatomist of power, J.M. Coetzee has created a body of work impressive for its vividness and restraint, for its immediacy and its enigmatic austerity, for its shapeliness and its intellectual courage. Writing out of a South African experience, with all its peculiar stresses and obsessions, he has resisted the easy moral posturings and false heroics that often disfigure dissident writing, and he has found a way to talk about the play of particular historical forces without limiting his perspective to a single time or country. A close student of oppression, brutality and injustice, he has taught his readers how to think about freedom and about the difficulties entailed in attempting to represent it.

Coetzee is someone, as he has said, "who has intimations of freedom (as every chained prisoner has)," and whose representations are never more than "shadows... of people slipping their chains and turning their faces to the light." To read him is to understand that nothing valuable is easy or conclusive, and that the writer himself, however passionate or full of conviction, must at present be painfully alert to the limitations of his own language. To get things right—so he has helped us to understand—, to feel adequate about our capacity to name and to judge, as one of his characters says, "you would need the tongue of a god." So he makes us believe, and so he makes us feel the weight of that difficult proposition.

In the early years of his professional writing life he did the kind of linguistic and stylistic analysis that would later inform several of his novels. He developed a sophisticated critique of naive realism and studied the impact of history upon the post-colonial writer. One thinks of him as the most theoretical of our great novelists, the one most interested in philosophical issues and capable of addressing them in narratives that never seem merely theoretical or arcane. For all that he has done to make his novels reflect an interest in issues of authority, gender, imperialism, indeterminacy, the fiction has always seemed to us remarkably human, sensual, intimate. Though deconstructionists and semioticians have a field day with his work, most of us—common readers—are grateful for the energy of his prose, the rhythms and surprises of his narrative, the disturbing suggestiveness of ideas that never seem superfluous or willed.

Of course it is tempting to speak of Coetzee as the master of a certain kind of fiction, but so various are his books, so eager has he been to take on fresh challenges, that one knows not quite how to describe him. Some speak of his academic precision, his analytic scruple. Others describe him as allegorist, psychologist, realist, ironist, post-modernist. Reviewers of *In The Heart of the Country* praised the biblical cadences of the prose, while later reviewers of *Waiting for the Barbarians* rightly praised its stark, spare, introspective intensities. In the novel *Foe* Coetzee moved away from the South Africa he explored in novels like *Age of Iron* and *Michael K* to offer a recasting of the Robinson Crusoe story, this one narrated by an eighteenth century Englishwoman obsessed with the mystery of one person's submission to another. In *The Master of Petersburg*, he dared to offer a fictional portrait of Dostoyevski, a figure so believably Dostoyevskian in its perversity and its combination of compassion and cruelty that at certain moments it seems to have been fashioned by Dostoyevski himself.

Of course Coetzee is interested, in his Russian novel, not merely in character or psychology but in exploring the very genesis of fiction. So, in *Michael K*, he is interested not simply in a person and a situation but in what one critic calls "the rules governing the production of... discourse." Though it is impossible to say what precisely a novel by J.M. Coetzee must look like or cover, we can say that each of his works is about many things—literary ideas and persons and politics—, and that no one of the works much resembles any other.

In short, we are moved by the range and the ferocity of Coetzee's imagination, by the shapeliness and torsion of his narratives, by the penetration of his political analysis and the cunning of his portraiture. Most of all, we are moved by the vision that informs everything he has written, a vision that goes—as Nadine Gordimer has memorably said—"to the nerve-centre of being" and enables Coetzee to find there "more than most people will ever know about themselves."

For his work and for his dedication to creative truth-telling, we honor J. M. Coetzee, and it is my privilege to present him for an honorary degree.

KATHRYN DAVIS [1996]

I first encountered Kathryn Davis as the author of short stories abundant in their invention and in their ability to make the ordinary seem full and potentially, occasionally, strange. I saw, also, in those early stories, signs of the linguistic range and intellectual weight that were to become distinguishing features of the two novels Kathryn has thus far given us.

What of those novels? The first, *Labrador*, was published in 1988; the second, *The Girl Who Trod on a Loaf*, was published in 1994. *Labrador* is a novel of two sisters coming of age in 1960's New Hampshire, a novel of the longing to break away and of the need to grow up without losing touch with the dark passions of adolescence. More than that, it is a work that constitutes, as one reviewer put it, "a fire-eater's act," a work of strange urgencies, off-center perspectives, and richly variegated surfaces. To note the poetically charged language of *Labrador*, its sometimes mythic resonances, is—properly—to suggest how much it is a work of the literary imagination, not a dutiful recording of formative experiences but a work of expansive energy and large creative ambition.

And if that is, at the least, what we must say of *Labrador*, then how much more must we remark the resplendence and the visionary breadth of *The Girl Who Trod on a Loaf*? Kathryn's second novel is, surely, the most extraordinary thing that she has done. It has been described, sometimes misleadingly, in several different ways. Some say it is a fairy tale, others that it is a philosophic novel. At least one reviewer calls it a feminist novel, another a stately—yes, stately—novel. Some say that, in its concern with opera, it approximates music, others that it is essentially a self-reflexive work, dwelling on its own "wheels and pulleys."

In fact, Kathryn's novel contains elements suggesting each of these accounts, but it is nowhere reducible to any one of them. A high-pitched narrative, to be sure, the novel is nonetheless a recognizable species of fiction, with realized characters, a sinuous but engaging plot design, and the patient attentiveness to setting and detail that we associate not with grand opera but with the nineteenth century novel. To be sure, Kathryn's book would perplex and astonish most nineteenth century readers of fiction, but its familiar novelistic features are handled with the skill and aplomb we associate with the masters of old-fashioned realism.

By what, precisely, would those hypothetical nineteenth century readers be perplexed and astonished? Perhaps by the sheer abundance of Kathryn's devices and metaphorical tropes, perhaps by the novel's unpredictable, sometimes chaotic movements between past and present, the ostensibly real and the probably imaginary. Of course, readers brought up on the extravagances of Dickens or the decidedly operatic fabulations of Stendhal would have no good reason to resist Kathryn's recitatives and ariettas. But who can tell? What we can say, for certain, is that Kathryn's novel offers god's plenty: that is to say, plenty of personality, esotericism, meditation, allusion, striving, mournfulness and intellectual repartee. And we can say, by the time we have completed Kathryn's novel, that we are invested in its characters and its ideas in ways we may not always have thought possible, so powerful was our attraction to the brilliant surfaces of her prose, to what one writer called its "high notes" and "striking chords." *The Girl Who Trod on a Loaf* is an exotic creation, but the reader who has no feeling for its dark probing of human need and disappointment is not the reader it deserves.

NICHOLAS DELBANCO [2001]

"Karl adds a spot of Naples yellow on the too-white shirt," we read early in Nick Delbanco's recent novel, *What Remains*. "He had primed the canvas with Siena and raw umber," the passage continues, ". . .but it makes the portrait somber, too serious this morning, and he wants to improve the mood of the picture and bring it up from too-great pessimism into the optimistic range of colors: yellow, a single spot of orange above his horn-rimmed glasses and, elsewhere, a bright green." The passage is characteristic Delbanco in its attention to mood and color, its alertness to vision and re-vision, its absorption in the perspective of a character entered confidently, intimately, but with more than a trace of reserve, as if to preserve some measure of wary, affectionate or at least sympathetic distance.

Nick has written many books—novels, story-collections, biographical group portraits, memoirs, travel books—and of course it is impossible to say that he does, each time out, a version of the same thing. That he is a wonderful and infinitely resourceful stylist no one has ever for a moment denied. An elegant, even mellifluous writer, he writes typically with a feeling for measure and pacing that seems to us entirely natural and unself-conscious, features that, in the hands of another writer, might well seem more deliberate. Yet there is, at the same time, in Nick's writing, what must be called an infusion of ripeness and abundance. His sentences are what one critic has called "prosperous with information and facts": "They owned a hedge with nests and gooseberry bushes and a gray Rolls Royce," reads an entirely characteristic sentence in Nick's 1970 novel, *News*. Or hear this: "So she gathers up her cane and shawl and magnifying glass and together they descend the stairs," we read in the recent novel, *What Remains*. So freely and copiously do the details multiply in the pages of Nick's work that we find ourselves craving them. Where, in the novels of other writers, the detail can seem an encumbrance, an obstacle to the building of momentum, in Nick's work, which is painterly and exquisitely textured, the detail provides much of the pleasure, and seems from the first an essential aspect of the writer's way of seeing. Just so, in this writing, there are interpolated bits of lore, snatches of song, occasional semantic observations, even brief corrections of diction in a fragment of a dialogue—as when *stupefying* is substituted, casually, in passing, for *stultifying*—though all of it feels in Nick's work comfortable, human, not at all artificial or pressurized.

The sentences in Nick's books unfold with a limpid beauty, quivering often with a sense of the fragility of things, alert to undercurrents, rustlings, unsaid but important meanings, conditional gestures. Nick has made room in his writing for improvisation, experiments, what is often referred to as a species of post-modern self-consciousness, though this is hardly what we routinely associate with his writing. He has reflected, in his fiction and in a variety of essays, on the difficulties of fiction-making, though he has seemed to mix memory and invention with little or no misgiving. There are, in Nick's mixed-media book, *The Lost Suitcase*, a number of epistemological teasers, lists with headings like thirteen ways of looking at a suitcase, thirteen ways of hiding a suitcase, and thirteen ways of looking for a suitcase, but Nick's books seem at last to proceed with a confident air, if not, ever, with a sense of stony finality or premature closure.

I know that Nick intends, this evening, to read to us from a new work of non-fiction, and of course there is much to say which I have not the time to say about his several previous non-fiction books. It is tempting, very much in brief, to suggest that the group of biographical portraits and the travel writing are distinguished by novelistic features, by character sketches, vivid place-settings, colorful anecdotes and brilliant antitheses. But in truth his book on the Beaux Arts Trio is not, finally, a novelistic work, and his book on the south of France, *Running in Place*, for all of its sensory lushness and its redolent snatches of dialogue, does not develop its material the way a Delbanco novel would. May it be sufficient to say that for his non-fiction writing as for his fiction, Nick has enlisted all of his faculties, that he has never seemed in his books to hug the shore, that he has never opted either for a false simplicity or for a false knowingness. With wit and refinement he has created works notable for their poise and their liveliness, their sometimes erratic particulars and the access they afford to a universe we wish, as imaginative beings, to inhabit.

ANITA DESAI [1994]

In reading the novels of Anita Desai one is tempted to impose upon them the categories on which literary academics inevitably rely. So we read *Fire On The Mountain* as a novel of old age, of decline and withdrawal. We read *Clear Light Of Day* as a family novel, or as a novel about tradition and modernity, and think glibly of the hectic and elusive *Baumgartner's Bombay* as at bottom a novel of dispossession and extraterritoriality. To such reductions and abuses are all good writers subjected. But the attempt, however understandable, is particularly inappropriate in the case of a writer so fine as Anita Desai, a writer so involved as she is in fingering the texture of our experience, in resisting the assimilation of everything to a clear, logically coherent pattern. In fact, Ms. Desai's capacity to thwart prediction, to elude pattern, even in what seem the most patterned and meticulous of novels, is a part of her great strength as a writer.

Here a brief example may be in order. As it happens, I've been teaching Anita Desai's *Clear Light Of Day* in a fiction course during the last two weeks. At an early point in our discussion I asked my students to assign sets of characteristics to opposing life patterns. On one side we would list the standard characteristics of a person who decided to stay at home in a traditional family enclave, preserving what she could while watching others of her family and friends go off to make new lives. On the other side we would list standard characteristics of a person who went off, leaving mother India behind and confronting the perils of modernity in Washington D.C. Those in this room who have read *Clear Light Of Day* will at once recognize that the principal characters of that novel correspond, very roughly, to the outline I have described, and that in both cases the "standard" characteristics associated with the life pattern do not fit the individual. If by "the one who stays" we mean one who is afraid of life, intellectually timid, and traditional rather than forward-looking in her view of things, then we must think again, since Ms. Desai's stay-at-home is in every way the more impressive and bracing of her characters. And if we typically associate the one who ventures forth with personal assertiveness, intellectual courage and repudiation of traditional supports, well then we are corrected again, since the ostensibly "modern" woman in *Clear Light Of Day* is neither tough-minded nor independent nor in any way impressive.

Ms. Desai takes no special or obvious pride in resisting our ordinary expectations. She makes no noisy or grandiose claims. She simply gives us whatever she can of character and milieu, helping us to speculate with her about what we cannot know, always assuming that there is more than our eye can take in, that even people who are eager to reveal themselves are more opaque than they suppose. With unfaltering deliberateness, in works that are—as Paul Scott put it—"beautifully shaped" and "infinitely moving," she gives us intense physical sensation and moral quandary, irony and sentiment.

Given the variety of Ms. Desai's work, which ranges from the sometimes hilarious satire of *In Custody* to the painful contemplativeness of *Fire On The Mountain* or the caustic disdain in passages of *Clear Light Of Day*, it is perhaps necessary to observe that, whatever she does, she does with respect for all that human beings can feel, for all that their thought can sometimes accommodate. In her hands everything is accorded its proper weight. Even small things matter; nothing is utterly trivial or inconsequential. Minor cruelties and casual betrayals are noted with the same precision lavished on the larger evils.

One also notes that Anita Desai is a magnificent prose writer, that she not only tells stories and creates memorable characters but again and again astonishes us with the versatility of her language and her control of emotional pitch. This is no small feat, no matter of fancy dress or metaphorical gimcrackery. Ms. Desai moves with a virtuoso's seeming ease from wit to tenderness, from operatic brilliance to astringent analysis, from feverish absorption to cool, even sometimes wicked detachment. This is a writer whose characters' "opposing thoughts collide in the dark like jittery bats in flight," for whom a character's anxious "pulse [may] beat in her temple, purple and bulbous," for whom an elderly woman may be caught, "standing at a height, like a beacon" and submitting to a younger person who "flung herself upon her friend and pecked and pecked her cold, flat cheek, crying little hideous cries of delight and love into the cringing ears."

Of such textures and tropes and intensifiers are the sentences of Anita Desai made. She is, as she has once said, a quiet writer, who admires—perhaps more than is warranted, some might say—the strenuous literary exertions of one Salman Rushdie. But she belongs, surely, among the relative handful of writers who have created indispensably refined, affecting, enigmatic works.

WILLIAM GASS [1994]

William Gass has spoken of the writer as "a true lie-minded man," and in that phrase he helps us to identify what is so very elusive in all of his work. For William Gass is bent on getting at the truth not as most of us understand it—not, that is, as the resolution of a problem presented to us as inhabitants of the ordinary world. He is interested in the truth that is made in response to problems that are made. He is interested not only in the truth of fiction but in the truth that is fiction. And this is a very special kind of truth, obviously, a truth, he says, that is not so much a way of viewing reality as an addition to reality. "The artist," Gass writes, "is not asked to construct an adequate philosophy, but a philosophically adequate world, a different matter altogether."

Most of us, of course, are not willing to grant to the writer quite that condition. When we read a great work of fiction, we do typically demand, if not an adequate philosophy, then at least a representation of the world that will allow us to believe we know it better than we did before. We demand, most of us, meanings that are useable, discussable, sensible; we demand characters that remind us of—people; and we applaud plot-lines that develop plausibly, in terms of what we have been given to expect by our own experiences.

William Gass challenges these demands, not because he believes that works of fiction don't stimulate thoughts of actual people, or plausible events, or useable meanings, but because our priorities are wrong. By looking to books mainly to have our expectations confirmed and our more modest appetites appeased, we shut ourselves off to other experiences that works of art can provide. We fail to note how, in a particular fiction, "The thought seems to grow a body," or how—and this is one of Gass's most memorable formulations—"a consciousness [may be] electrified by beauty."

Fortunately, William Gass has written several works of fiction that demonstrate the different things that a great novel or story can do. And he has written many essays on the nature of the art he and others like him practice.

The essays are collected in several volumes, and represent to many of us the furthest and most gratifying reaches of the essay form. The fiction includes a novel of great genius, entitled *Omensetter's Luck*; a collection of stories, *In the Heart of the Heart of the Country*, which contains several unforgettable items, most especially "The Pederson Kid"; a bravura mixed-media work called *Willie Masters Lonesome Wife*; and an enormous, electrifying, sometimes bewildering novel called *The Tunnel*, published last year. *Omensetter* is without the typographic puns and lunacies of *Willie Masters*; the stories are mostly without those teeming barrages of verbiage that one associates with Bill Gass generally; *The Tunnel*, at least in its opening sections, refuses the odd, though mostly linear narrative continuity of *Omensetter*. All of which is to say that it's never been easy to know exactly what Bill Gass has been up to. We think of words like opulence and flamboyance and intellectual hi-jinx to describe the work, but we find also what Bill himself calls concept, order and proportion. Some critics have failed to see in Bill's latest book what they expected from the author of *Omensetter's Luck*, but we see in it not only order but reach, audacity, genius.

More precisely, and suggestively, we see in it, truly see, everything its author wishes us to see, or hear, or smell, or taste, with a vividness, an immediacy, a shock of recognition altogether rare. The sky in Gass doesn't simply "recede;" it recedes "like an illustration in a physics book." Sparrows don't simply chirp or chatter; they "quarrel and complain." The soda bottles don't simply stand in the refrigerator; they are observed "shivering in the door of the fridge." Casanova was not merely a lover; he was the man "to whom truth was the ardent center of a tossed skirt." These examples, drawn from but a single page of *The Tunnel*, perhaps convey, in some tiny measure, the teeming fecundity of Bill Gass's imagination and the unstoppable ripeness of his prose.

Whatever the debates stirred by *The Tunnel*, and whatever strikes us as most compelling and memorable in Bill Gass's work generally, we are surely inspired to say of it that here, truly, is God's and Gass's plenty.

NADINE GORDIMER [1991]

Nadine Gordimer is, of course, one of our greatest writers, the author of ten novels and seven collections of short stories and a critic not only of apartheid but of many forms of systemic violence and oppression. She is also, as many of us well know, our most effective instructor in the limitations and the indispensable benefits of liberalism. Often described as a radical thinker—nowhere more powerfully than in her fiction—she has, on more than one occasion, reminded us that literature at its best is more than, certainly different from, the sum of its ideas and convictions. And yet she is a radical thinker, and her novels are nowhere subordinated to the simple promulgation of ideas, political or otherwise.

From the time of her first novel, *The Lying Days*, published in 1953, through such famous later works as *Burger's Daughter*, *July's People*, and A *Sport of Nature*, she has studied mainly her own South African society in its hope and decline, activist renewal and neo-fascist nationalism. She has used the novel as a means of inquiring into the past and future prospects of her country, and she has taught countless readers to understand that what happens in South Africa is of tremendous importance to all of us, and that neither slogans nor platitudes can help us to deal with problems so daunting as those she portrays. She has taught us, that is to say, that conflict is in the grain of human relations, and that there is no such thing as a universalist politics or a coherent position that will satisfy everyone.

But of course it is a little misleading to speak of Nadine Gordimer principally as a political writer and radical intellectual, however often she must come before us as a political spokesperson or concerned citizen. Principally, after all, she is a great and greatly ambitious writer, one who has driven the shorter fictional forms in new directions and who has created an authentically new novel that operates both as an instrument of knowledge and as a generator of the deepest feelings. The critic Elizabeth Hardwick has rightly spoken of the variety of things we learn in Gordimer's fiction, the way "things are grown and harvested," "how, exactly, a power station is blown up," and what it means "to be a black girl discovered with a white man." Hardwick is also helpful in saying that Gordimer's work "is a vast discourse on everything the vast scene provides," but more important by far are the words she uses to conclude that observation, namely, that "the scene itself [is] a landscape created by a majestic imagination." For all that Gordimer shows us about the world, for all that she helps us to understand about ourselves and others, it is a created, an imagined, landscape that we confront in her work. Hers is in essence—surely this is too obvious to say—an activity of imagination. Though we are instructed by her work, what it offers most unmistakably is an instruction not in correct political attitudes or positions but in ways of imagining reality.

What this means, clearly, is that when Gordimer gives us character, she gives us figures we can alternately understand and be puzzled by, figures who can inspire affection but who are drawn with no trace of sentimentality or needless exaggeration, figures who—if they are victims—convey no sanctity about their suffering, and who—if they are oppressors—are always more than abstract symbols of evil. When she gives us situation, it is situation alive with the possibility of change, for better or for worse, situation that exists not as an inert datum but in complex interaction with the exertion and will of characters who act even as they are acted upon. When Gordimer gives us metaphor, image, analogy, paradox, she gives them not as tokens of a desire to glibly transcend the constraints of ordinary language but as part of a medium of thought so fraught with ambivalence, so burdened with contradiction, that it can register its vacillations only in a language that is free to do what it must.

As a community of grateful readers many of whom—teachers and students alike—have actually studied and written about the work of Nadine Gordimer, and who have learned from it the ways of the educated imagination, we are proud to offer her an honorary degree as a sign of our enduring admiration.

MARY GORDON [1997]

Mary Gordon writes about many things, but she has identified her primary subject as "family happiness," "daily rhythms," rather than "the music of the spheres." This, she says, her father would have thought "a stubborn predilection for the minor," though her mother knew better. And of course there is in those distinctions, between the quotidian and the cosmic, the minor and the major, the feminine and the masculine, more than a little to think about. For at least fifteen years now no one has been chewing on such issues more provocatively than Mary Gordon. She takes them up in brilliant polemical essays, in sharp-eyed book reviews, in memoiristic pieces and books, and in a wide range of fictions.

But I prefer not to think of Mary as a novelist of families, though I love family novels and think of hers often as moving over the very ground covered by other such "minor" writers as William Trevor and the Christina Stead who gave us *The Man Who Loved Children*. The truth is, Mary not only writes about many subjects, but does so with such conviction and absorption that it is hard not to associate her more or less exclusively with each of the themes she embraces.

In recent years Mary has been very much involved with a memoiristic book about her father, entitled *The Shadow Man*. This is a book about lies and deception, about love and disillusion and finding a way back. It is a book filled with patient discovery and relentless probing. "Facts nose their way into what I thought was the past like a dog sticking his nose under a lady's skirts," Mary writes. "How I resent the insidious, relentless, somehow filthy nudging of the facts." The reader who follows her discoveries, astonished, bemused, occasionally repulsed, can only marvel at Mary's persistent good will, her refusal of righteous indignation, her moral sternness and sense of the ridiculous. Relentless in her will to uncover, she remains at once dispassionate and merciful.

In fact, in all of her writing Mary has been an exemplary truth-teller, often assertive, witty, and always clear. The sentences bite, deepen, surprise. "We go into the ninth grade English class," she writes in a memoir, "and I am impressed by the teacher, who speaks to her students of Dickens with the passion of someone who has taught less than two years." In another piece she corrects a misconception about the Irish. Yes, she writes, "they love to talk, but they don't like to tell you anything. So if you're happy to have a good time and listen to the shape of the language itself, you'll have a wonderful time talking to an Irishman."

But I want to end this introduction with a little passage from a reflection of Mary's on Warhol, who "says to everything I could possibly say: bullshit. But he wouldn't say that, it wouldn't be pretty or cool to say that; what he says is worse, much worse. What he says is it doesn't matter. It could be anything. Anything could be anything. One thing or another." It is Mary's sense that there is something awful and cruel in Warhol, her sense that things really do matter, including things that make us laugh, things that are small or painful or absurd, that makes Mary Gordon one of our most affecting and scrupulous writers.

MARY GORDON [2001]

Though Mary Gordon's writing has moved me and instructed me and provoked me in the course of the twenty or more years since I first began to read her, I have lately thought of her as a brilliant comic writer. This has, no doubt about it, something to do with her novel *Spending*, which had us laughing as we read it, and laughing again later on as we thought of Mary herself delighting in the invention of this or that deliciously wanton or extravagant sequence. An unbuttoned, one is tempted to call it Rabelaisean, work of the imagination, *Spending* is comic not only in its witty turns and situational invention, but in its sheer appetite for excess, the ease with which it extends its limbs so as to go, more than occasionally, deftly over the top.

But Mary has always displayed a gift for comedy, even where her work has been intensely serious or downright grim. In her novels, as well as in her essays and memoiristic writing, we find a finely calibrated feeling for the preposterous, an alertness to deceptions and disfigurements that bedevil apparently simple or straightforward relationships. Even where the emotions at large in one of Mary's fictional households are tentative, uneasy, we are alerted to the prospect of something odd, some epitomizing gesture or verbal slip that captures, just so, the essential absurdity of a relationship otherwise gray and commonplace in its apparent features. This sort of thing, for which a reader is ever grateful, is the more remarkable because it consorts so well with other ostensibly incompatible features of Mary's work, with her gift for polemic intensities, for moral and spiritual reflection.

Mary's comic predilections are especially well represented in the recent non-fiction. There an uncommon gift for portraiture, by turns tender and malevolent, releases in the prose a delicate mix of melancholy and acidulous eloquence. Love and disillusionment often consort very closely in Mary's writing, and though she has not much appetite for complaint or lamentation, she is a mordant satirist, an anatomist of petty cruelties and deceptions whose very pettiness seems to us painfully funny. No reader of Mary's memoirs will forget the smallness, the oppressive airlessness of the domestic interiors she evokes or the gray dessicated lives of some of their inhabitants. The wonder of it is that, from the minor cruelties and standard desolations of Mary's people, there emerges, steadily, an appreciation of comic insufficiencies, thwarted intimacies so perfectly familiar as to seem mildly hilarious.

Equally remarkable is that, with an eye trained to note the absurd, the absurdly inconsequential, the wheedling, the unctuous, Mary nonetheless maintains a passionate curiosity, a feeling for what she calls "unbreakable eternal silences" and for the miraculous. A comedian poised at or near the lip of many a quotidian abyss, Mary invites us, all the same, to participate with her in the pursuit of revelations large and small. Amused often at her own " Jamesian" wide-eyed innocence, her hunger for significance and complication and suffering, at her capacity for "awe" and "reverence," she is the most improbable of comic writers, one whose gift seems often as surprising to her as to us, whose gift is a combination of candor, timing, an inexhaustible capacity for wonder, and sheer intellectual play.

I don't know, of course, exactly what Mary has in store for us this evening, and it's possible that, by design, she won't have us laughing, not this time. But if you doubt me, well, have a look, for starters, at the essay on "Rome: The Visible City" in Mary's recent book, *Seeing Through Places*. And then, please, move on to Mary's memoir, *The Shadow Man*, passing without pause to one or more of the novels. Further detailed recommendations to follow upon request.

MAUREEN HOWARD [1999]

At a PEN evening in New York City two winters ago, Susan Sontag introduced Maureen Howard as a great writer whose works are enormously pleasure-giving while making considerable demands that many worthy readers are prepared to negotiate. Another way of saying this is suggested by the word "original," as in—"Maureen Howard is a true original," which is to say, a writer who uses the full resources of the language and of her chosen medium to make something new and surprising. The author of seven novels and a National Book Critics Circle Award-winning memoir entitled *Facts of Life*, Maureen has inspired many of our best writers and critics, from Russell Banks to Richard Poirier, from Bill Kennedy to Alfred Kazin, who compare what she has done with Bridgeport, Connecticut to Joyce's work with Dublin, declaring that she writes "with some of Joyce's meticulous and sure abundance," praising her rare command of music and substance, history and the present shifting moment.

For a faithful reader most especially infatuated with Maureen's two most recent novels, *Natural History* and *A Lover's Almanac*, the word that comes most immediately to mind—so I would contend—is *design*: design, as in the weaving, say, of a sumptuous tapestry, where mind and eye are constantly arrested by pleasing and provocative arrangements of words and passages. In Maureen's writing a character will develop as richly and complexly as one could wish, but a reader is likely to be moved as well by the painterly detail expended on the setting forth, the deft, delicate strokes everywhere scoring the surfaces of Maureen's prose, the subtly managed contrasts—as between what a character seemed and what a character was. Though it is possible to find, in re-

164

views of Maureen's fiction, praise for her "sharp" dialogue and her "storytelling immediacy"—I've taken those phrases from a *New York Times Book Review* of 1992—the praises I've cited are, all of them, somewhat misleading in directing us to virtues not at all peculiar to Maureen and not at all associated with her great, original strengths. To think instead of design in Maureen's work is to come nearer to her remarkable virtuosity and her stylistic audacity.

Maureen pushes, tests the line between prose and the music of poetry. She is never timid about her music, investing her lines with a wide, sometimes dazzling range of colors and tonal effects, internal chimings and alliterations. She is not uneasy about a page on which we read of a woman "strutting in stiletto heels" who "paps her pearly breasts," in a "loft littered," and, well, you get the idea. This is not the plain style, clearly, though Maureen's instinct for placing flowers in the buttonholes of her prose is always beautifully controlled, and her sentences are often enough lean and serviceable, the speed of her evolving narrative more or less unimpeded.

Of course it is possible to speak about Maureen's work in the more familiar terms used to describe successful works of fiction, to speak of her vivid portrayal of manners and morals, her mastery of American speech idiom, her sure understanding of ambition and striving and the means required by most persons to rise in the world and make more of themselves than they thought they would. But though we do very much admire Maureen's vision of American life, her sense of what is restless and corrupting and inventive and renewing in our culture, we are as readers relentlessly drawn to the intricately renewing refreshments of her writing itself. What in other writers might well seem a surfeit of devices and tropes is in Maureen an ever-impressive manifest of urgent skill and invention. We note the profusion in this work not only of tonal elements but of proliferating visual complements, sometimes including fanciful diagrams, drawings, italicized passages, surprising interpolations. In *A Lover's Almanac*, Benjamin Franklin suddenly and briefly emerges as a full-blown character strangely setting off aspects of the contemporary character with whom he is associated. There is nothing in this juxtaposition that is anything but delightful and enlarging, and we note—as always in Maureen's work—the scrupulous deployment of relevant details to create an abiding impression of historical density, the past subtly interanimating the present.

In fact, Maureen Howard has given us the virtuosity we find only in our best writers, a body of work—as one critic has said—"always in the midst of breaking free of itself," embodying variety and contradiction and abundance.

WILLIAM KENNEDY [1999]

Many of us, writers and professors and readers, convened in downtown Albany a few months back to celebrate Bill Kennedy and watch him receive a new state award for his work. It was a grand evening, with more than a few hilarious moments. The tributes were thick in the spring air, with only a little muddle to distract us from the essential magnitude of the work, and the writer, we were there to think about. Like others present, I suppose, I let the public words roll pleasurably over me, doing my best to hold in mind all the while the rich cadences of Bill's prose, its prodigious delicacies and turns of wit, such as I've known them as a reader over twenty years. But then I heard one of the distinguished writer-speakers refer, with becoming conviction and solemnity, to Bill as a wonderful writer of plain prose, and Nick Delbanco and I, seated together in the audience, looked at each other and silently, wordlessly asked what the hell the word *plain* can mean when applied to the work of Bill Kennedy. Of course the epithet was intended, no doubt about it, as a compliment, as in the case of a man who knows how to go about his literary business without undue distraction by the presumably superfluous niceties of the written language. And of course compliments are generally. . . nice, but in this case the particular characterization was—no doubt about it, just a little misleading, and so I thought, well, not much chance of leaping to my feet in the grand ballroom in downtown Albany, commandeering the microphone, and making an essential correction. But there is, after all, so I thought, Saratoga in July. There is always Saratoga, and Bill Kennedy, in July.

When I think of Bill's writing, I think sometimes of the

poet Robert Lowell's tribute to his poet friend John Berryman. We used the language as if we'd made it, Lowell rightly said, and that is often the way we feel about the language as it seethes and charms and incites and mourns in Bill's novels. It is not only Bill's stories that are spell-binding but his language. No reader—or almost no reader—can miss in Bill's work the presence of a richly inflected idiom, the sheer delight this writer takes in seeing and coloring, with a vividness few American writers have approached. This is not an achievement that has anything essentially to do with odd words, arcane references, though Bill has known how to appropriate nineteenth century rhetoric in *Quinn's Book*, and to put into the mouths of various characters in various novels the music appropriate to their time and station. The achievement has more to do with the characteristically active quality of Bill's prose, its lively pulse, its casual grace notes and propulsive energy, the sense it gives that it is in the service of character and idea and narrative while at the same time it is bound to light sparks, to make its own way, not simply to use the common language in the plain ways typically available to, and good enough for, most of us. There is nothing remotely ostentatious about Bill's linguistic invention, nothing pretty or fussy about his grace or diction. He does go about his novelistic business with a clear-sighted air and a brisk confidence, but his is an unconstraining voice, and he wouldn't know how to write dead or uninteresting sentences if he tried. So it seems.

The outlines of Bill Kennedy's project are by now about as familiar as the story of his career, his writer's obstructed progress through *Ironweed* and the novels that followed in its wake. Central to the project, of course, is the creation of a large, multigenerational, turbulently eventful and coherent novelistic world, a world in which places and people crop up again and again, in which recurrent patterns of concern and behavior assume a steady, growing importance. Bill's northeastern, mostly Albany-centered urban landscape has been compared to the fictional world created by William Faulkner in the American South, James Joyce in Dublin and Balzac in 19th century France, and though such comparisons are useful only in defining one kind of resemblance, the company is very good, and any writer would be more than a little pleased to reside in such a neighborhood.

Bill's Albany, of course, is not simply a small upstate city but—as others have noted—the "universal city" of his imagination, the place where fate and chance conspire to produce the believable and the believably fantastic. The action varies wildly, from the boxing ring to the bar room, from the theater to the political clubhouse and the drawing room, from the marital bedroom to the flophouse. And just as we expect variety of incident and abundance of character in Bill, so too do we expect, and get, an abundance of ideas, from the complex analysis of power and sanctimony to the relation between guilt and destitution. Like the best fictionists, Bill keeps lots of ideas and actions circulating, and never—to shift the metaphor—never drops the thread. And of course the creation of his large and generous fictional world is powered by a language that is never less than bright, a source of inexhaustible readerly pleasures.

WILLIAM KENNEDY [2000]

Bill Kennedy will read tonight from the manuscript of a new novel, which I haven't read as yet and can't discuss. But last weekend I went back to Bill's most recent published novel, *The Flaming Corsage*, from 1996, and I thought again about what makes it so satisfying and audacious, and so utterly characteristic of Bill's work. Of course, like the new novel Bill will read from tonight, it is a part of Bill's ongoing Albany cycle, and of course it sets in motion a various cast of characters, some of them new to the cycle, others familiar to us from earlier novels like *Ironweed*. Just so, *The Flaming Corsage* delivers much that the earlier novels have taught us to expect from so consistently lavish a writer: sharply imagined sequences, extended swathes of racy dialogue, intensities and near-digressions, local color and eloquent, affecting retrospection. The action veers steadily, from the theatrical to the naturalistic, the angle of vision now close-up, now just a little bit detached, as for philosophic reflection or speculation. This is a writer, we are reminded, who can move comfortably in a single page from underwear and chicken fat to the language of destiny, the everlasting, guilt, and "the great cipher."

But the critic Harold Bloom was surely right to observe that in *The Flaming Corsage* Bill "demonstrates an aesthetic exuberance beyond his previous work." This is no small thing, as is evident to anyone who has regarded the aesthetic exuberance of Bill's previous novels as one of their most attractive features. Bill has never seemed to us a straight-ahead realist writer with a moderate, workmanlike relationship to language. Often he has seemed to bend, fiercely bend the language to very special purposes. Often he has invented an arch diction, a deliberately literary or archaic syntax, a carefully heightened prose befitting his material. If aesthetic exuberance in *The Flaming Corsage* is yet more considerable, well, then Bill has risked more than ever before, and he has come through in a way that safer writers are not likely ever to taste.

What does aesthetic exuberance look like in a novel by Bill Kennedy? At the sentence level it is observable in a certain lushness that is apt to seem a little bit put on for the occasion, as in the following: "Here were the wellsprings of power and wealth that had gilded the heart, soul, and lifetime of Katrina Taylor, weeping child of the new century, wounded by the flames of hellish flowers, who can now find no substitute in life for her loss, her diminishment, her abasement." That is not the end of Bill's sentence, but you get the idea, note the lavishness of the prose, the unabashed theatricality of the metaphor (as in "flames of hellish flowers"), the refusal to be satisfied with the single word *loss* when *diminishment* and *abasement* can be added to it.

This lavishness, this deliberate display of controlled excess, is so striking and effective, of course, only because it fits the setting, period and circumstance it serves. More especially, the prose is deployed in a book that is some of the time spare and fastidious, which reads now and then like a treatment for a play or, as one critic noted, "something between evidence and journalism, [even] a police blotter."

But the aesthetic exuberance is also discernible in Bill's use of dramatic placard titles to announce the discontinuous, non-linear tableaux that are the chosen, inspired form of this novel, titles like "Katrina Ruminates on What She Has Seen" or "The Rape of Felicity: Two Versions." This device, together with the use of brief interludes that read like newspaper reviews, or the dialogue from a play script, or pages from a diary, make the novel ceaselessly new, so that we are ever surprised by its unrepentant venturesomeness, and marvel at its ability to sustain narrative momentum while undertaking so many formal innovations.

Often before I've spoken, like many others, about Bill's capacity to treat the Albany of his imagination not only as an actual place at various actual times but to transform it into a sort of "universal city"—not my expression, alas—where the believable and the believably fantastic conspire. This is as true of *The Flaming Corsage* as of *Ironweed* and *Quinn's Book* and the other works Bill has given us. For all of Bill's obvious gifts as a storyteller and world-creator and portrait painter, for all of his aesthetic exuberance, he is also a writer of enormous grace and tact.

BERNARD MALAMUD [1982]

When his novel, *Dubin's Lives*, came out a year or two ago, I sent Bernard Malamud a note to say that I hadn't yet figured out how the man who wrote *The Assistant* and *The Fixer* and the stories in *The Magic Barrel* had managed also to write so Lawrentian a book as his most recent novel. Then I sat next to Bern at a dinner party a month or two later and he said, among other things, more or less the following: first, that a book in which Lawrence himself figures as some sort of presence is not by that token clearly a Lawrentian novel; second, that I was perhaps too sure I knew what kind of writer he was, based on my first encounter with his stories and with an early novel that was hardly, after all, the only kind of novel he'd written. Maybe, Bern suggested, *Dubin's Lives* was not an anomalous work. Maybe it was only the latest installment in the career of a writer unusually restless, who'd produced a tragi-comic baseball novel, an academic novel, a historical novel, and other works bound to surprise anyone who thought of him simply as one of the so-called Hart, Schaffner and Marx trio of American-Jewish fictionists—Saul Bellow's term, not mine—who'd won a large following in the fifties and sixties, and whose Jewishness seemed to many readers the central inescapable feature of their writerly identities.

Of course it's true that Bern has written in several different literary registers and fictional genres, but it is equally true that he has done, more or less consistently, the series of different things that nonetheless betray his characteristic obsessions and his abiding moral temperament. He does not write a patently sophisticated, smart, preening prose. His sentences are hard-won, never heavy, but often harsh, bitten off, as if written under pressure, through clenched teeth. Whatever the subject matter, whether story or novel, the work has a genuine style, feels at every moment like a made thing, though at the same time it is without affectation, urgent even while moving slowly over a small square of turf. There is no fear, no apparent fear, of intensity, no aversion to exacerbation. "You pipsqueak nothing. I'll freeze you to pieces," one character hisses at a companion. Another, opening a door, is "like a corpse adjusting his coffin lid." Characters spray curses, rise in wrath, turn to reveal a face or a mouth "like iron." Passages from *Dubin's Lives* resonate with a different kind of intensity, to be sure, but with a more or less comparable sense that matters of life and death, of the greatest moral and emotional urgency, are at stake.

If I take my examples here, and much of my direction, from the short fiction, that is a consequence of Bern's decision to read to us this evening an early story, and also of his willingness to participate tomorrow with a good part of this academic audience in a lengthy discussion built around five of his stories, which we have read together in preparation for this visit.

Of the stories in general we may say that they are at once grim and exhilarating. The exhilaration we feel is a function of two features primarily: first, a kind of wit that is more than a little wild, sometimes nutty. This wit informs a free untrammeled invention which is as comfortable with whimsy as with hallucination and dark, absurdist fable. Examples abound, though not one by itself seems remotely sufficient to suggest the abundance and variety of Malamud's wit.

The second feature is a gift for unpredictable verbal eruptions. We see rather little of this in a novel like *The Assistant*, where, as Leslie Fiedler has written, the art has much to do with "discipline and self-denial," with the seemingly "perverse" decision to withhold as much as possible any expression of "the poetry of banal lives." But in the stories grayness yields more or less persistently to color and surprise, to small, sometimes rough felicities. A cough is "brutal." In a dank, cold basement apartment a "bony goldfish" is observed "thrashing its frigid tail" in "arctic seas." A nighttime walk to the subway is "tedious." Everywhere the language seems fresh, even where the quotidian predominates and the speakers themselves are without what typically passes for eloquence. "It's an old-fashioned language they don't use it nowadays," says the character Davidov in the story "Take Pity," and though the run-on formulation by no means describes Malamud's language, which is never "old-fashioned" even when characters drop into Yiddish inflections or old-world dialects, it is surely true to say that the language of Malamud's fiction is not used by anyone "nowadays," and never was used by anyone in the past.

It may well be that Bern's primary contribution to our literature will seem, in the end, to involve his sustained re-visioning of Jewishness as a moral response-system—though system is probably the wrong word here—that is as available to gentiles as to Jews. But I prefer to think of him as a writer who has invented a number of rhetorics and decidedly incompatible worlds in the pursuit of what he would call, with no embarrassment or apology, aesthetic pleasure and a complex view of the life we lead. "Art celebrates life," Bern has said on more than one occasion, and though, most often, I resist and mistrust such formulations, when I read and re-read Bern's stories and novels, I believe him.

NORMAN MANEA [2000]

In one of the unforgettable novellas collected in Norman Manea's book *Compulsory Happiness*, a character suddenly erupts with a barrage of questions, all of them facing in the same terrible direction. "Anyone, anything, that's it, that's the explanation? Anyone can do anything, feel anything, any time, toward anyone, that's the idea... we're all alike, no exceptions?" The thought contained in these questions is by no means exceptional in the works of Norman Manea, works which reflect his primary training during World War II at the Transnistria concentration camp where he was interned, from age five to nine, by the Romanian fascist regime, and also reflect, yet more insistently, his secondary education as an adult in the communist Romania of Ceasescu.

This is in no way to suggest that Norman is, in the obvious sense of the term, a dissident writer. Typically the commissars or torturers in his work are very human. They sneeze, dab at their watery eyes, confess to weakness, say witty things. One particularly repulsive figure in a work called "The Interrogation" offers gifts to the brutalized woman he interrogates and croons to her "I'm courting you the old-fashioned way, so to speak. Being considerate of ladies who honor me with their kind attention." By turns hysterical and pathetic, vicious and solicitous, this example of the system in which Norman spent much of his adult life seems to us, exactly as Norman's character has it, capable of anything any time, so that to speak of explanation is to speak, finally, of nothing, and everything. The dissident writer must write out of the conviction that things are at least a little clearer than they seem in Norman's work, and that the efforts of like-minded men and women can conceivably make the particular place and time

176

better than they are. Norman's business as a writer is not with that hope, that prospect.

There is, of course, as we try to think about such things, the matter of temperament to contend with, and Philip Roth was surely on to something some years ago when he wrote that Norman's "thoughtfulness, his intellectual subtlety and his affection for complexity, his quiet wit—even his taste for life's every day pleasures are not necessarily the best weapons against institutionalized thuggery." All true. And yet, strangely, Norman's has been one of the most powerful voices ever to come out of the nightmare worlds he revisits again and again in his fiction. With no desire for abrasive confrontation, with none of the standard dissident attraction to the making of theatrical scenes, Norman has brought to life a world largely remote from the quieter world most of us have known, and he has found a way—many ways— to press us—yes, even us, the soft ones—to think about our own vulnerability to terror and betrayal, our capacity for humiliation and infantilization. Consistently, in fact, Norman teaches us very simply, without a trace of didacticism, with gusts of wild, uncanny humor, what it means to be human, not heroic, but stubbornly resistant wherever possible to stupidity and viciousness.

So that we find it in ourselves to say, a little sheepishly perhaps, no, not all alike, not all stupid and vicious, not every one "perfectly capable," as he says, "of kissing the devil's ass."

NORMAN MANEA [2001]

In recent months I've been reading and re-reading portions of Norman Manea's lengthy, recently completed, memoir. I say portions because Norman writes in Rumanian and most of the memoir has yet to be translated. Particularly interesting, to one reader at least, is the voice that sounds through this new work, for it calls to mind a voice we hear more than occasionally in Norman's fiction. Not easy, of course, to define that voice, to give it a name. Quiet, or modest, or diffident: none of these, certainly not any one by itself, will do, no more than subtle, which perhaps suggests that Norman aims to be subtle, that subtlety is a manner he puts on. Better to say, probably, that the voice in the work is tentative, not timid, that it is wary of theatrical effect, but stained all the same with a wash of color, variegated, modulated in dark hues.

Of course you'll soon hear for yourselves—in the story Norman will read—the voice I'm trying to describe. It will reverberate, softly, with the unmistakable traces of Norman's characteristic lyricism, a lyricism restrained but inexorable. It's obvious in small things, in a sentence fragment that is built to achieve a modest surging effect, like "To cast himself into the deep, even deeper, purged, healed of the last traces of this wound." It is present in a phrase, in the odd, almost slack sequence that culminates in a casual oxymoron, as in "the sea flows more and more slowly, calmly, freely, a tender annihilation." Those final words, "tender annihilation," might almost be said to capture, exactly, the mood that is so much a part of Norman's voice, a voice in which tenderness persists even where the burden of the discourse is the annihilation witnessed, suffered by this writer and his several fictional counterparts.

To be sure, tenderness itself is often suspect in Norman's writing. He is wary even of the all-too-human gesture, the mild confidence or intimate touch of a hand. The man who reveals a weakness, offers a condolence, avows a fellow-feeling, Norman suggests, may well have a weapon in his glove, a savage confederate at the door, a predatory design he wishes to effect. Tenderness is no refuge against savagery, we come gradually to see, and no reliable gauge of intention or actual feeling. Subtlety in Norman's work is often a function of his preternatural wariness, his alertness to treachery, duplicity, terror.

As many in this room well know, as readers of Norman's books and as members of previous Writers Institute audiences, Norman's life experience accounts at least in part for the substance of his alertness. His fiction often engages his previous lives, as resident of the Transnitria concentration camp in World War II, and later as an adult in the Communist Rumania of Ceasescu, who was finally deposed about a decade ago, just after Norman and his wife Cella finally got out of their country and arrived in New York.

Of course, as I've said before in introducing Norman, the background information ought in no way to suggest that Norman is a dissident writer—not in the ways ordinarily suggested by the word dissident. Norman's outlook is too complex for straightforward dissidence, his temperament too melancholy to allow for any note in his work of stridency or didacticism. The memoiristic work that he has been composing is, in this respect, very telling, for it conveys perfectly that wry melancholy in Norman's writing, that gift for the perfectly telling detail or locution, the willing ness to risk everything on a sudden brief swerve into eloquence or Proustian nostalgia or an unaccustomed severity, lifting almost unaccountably above the apparently placid surface of the prose. Nothing could be further from polemic than this writing of Norman's, though in his essays—a number collected in the volume *On Clowns*—he demonstrates that he is not altogether averse to stricture and exposé. The true note of his creative writing, though, is the accent you are about to hear for yourselves.

I'm tempted, of course, to share with this audience my favorite passages of Norman's writing, to dwell, however briefly, on what he calles the "stale clichés" of "other seasons," the "sticky pulsing plasma" of unfamiliar sexual encounters, the slow, fatal entry into ordinariness, also known as "the ranks of banality," the "mysticism of meaninglessness" experienced by so many of Norman's characters who are inured to "the uncanny atmosphere of unreality" in Ceasescu's Romania. But I'll step reluctantly aside and ask you please to welcome the man who can best produce the voice that has taken up permanent residence in many an ear over the last decade, a voice at once troubling and brotherly, as Philip Roth once said, wry and quietly inexorable.

JAY McINERNEY [2001]

From the beginning, which is to say, roughly twenty years ago, Jay McInerney seemed to his contemporaries the ideal chronicler of a life associated with the words *fast, edge, waste,* and *excess.* He was, it seemed, the very perfect spiritual incarnation of a particular cultural moment, his novelistic style itself a hip embodiment of the world he brought to life. Often overlooked, of course, even in the enthusiastic notices received by his novel *Bright Lights, Big City,* was the fact that Jay's early works did more than bring the subculture of druggy, yuppie, early-eighties Manhattan to life. His novels were by no means celebrations of excess, though they were imbued with an insider's sense of the excitement and frenzy, the rage to get and be high, that gave Jay's works their authority. But it was clear to many readers intoxicated by the sheer surface brilliance of Jay's prose and impressed by his adept gamesman's command of the cultural terrain that Jay was in fact a punishing satirist, a comedian of manners, a new breed of writerly social critic. What appeared to be a comfortable pact between the writer and his material, a kind of mutuality of outlook as between the controlling authorial intelligence and his characters, turned out to be, should have appeared from the first to be, a very uneasy alliance. The critic of manners and mores knew himself to be heavily invested in the milieu he examined, but the novels he wrote were themselves vehicles of necessary engagement and disengagement, intimacy and recoil.

With some writers the words *surface brilliance* seem more or less appropriately to suggest *mere* surface brilliance. The critic James Wood describes the "harmless, puffy lyricism" of a certain kind of showy prose, the showy writer in this case "a very rich man...adding a lazy ten percent to each sentence." Nothing could be further from the writing of Jay McInerney, whose effects are never puffy, never lazy, never a mere gratuity. Jay's brilliances are, to be sure, out there, relentlessly coming at us, though the pacing is never less than expert, and allowance is made for the setting up and exposition or plain unfussy character development without which there can be no authentic novelistic experience. Often the effects are principally what might well be called effects of wit, where the wit is unmistakably in the service of illumination.

"A head taller than me," the narrator says of his adolescent patrician friend early in Jay's novel, The Last of the Savages, "with shaggy dark hair, he wore ripped khakis and a much worn button-down shirt, the tail of which flapped behind him; he suffered his clothing the way you might inhabit an old summer cottage, cheerfully indifferent to the sagging porch and peeling paint." Wonderful lines, you want to say, the mark of a genuine writer. But as you read on in Jay's novel, you discover that such writing is by no means exceptional, that it is a defining mark of Jay's fiction, central to its character and its distinction. No ten percent gratuity here. Here the style is a manifest of the work's very substance and of its claim upon us.

Another word often used to speak of Jay is *smart*, and again, it is a word that can be misleading, as where the word is intended to say glib, all-too-knowing, wearing one's irony like a badge. In fact, Jay's ironies are multiple, various in their targets and in their several kinds, and not at all compulsive. The comedy in Jay's fiction is sometimes broad, but it never descends to caricature—the odd Southern aristocrats in The Last of the Savages are fully human, and the Mississippi Delta Negroes, "sullen" and "slouched" or caught in their "suspicious insouciance," are never blunted by habitual gestures or uniform speech patterns. The

Southern working-class houses are populated, to be sure, by familiar working-class types, but they are brought powerfully to life by the novelist's extraordinary grasp of setting and denizen: "You sometimes sensed," Jay writes, "the male animal in the background, torpid and menacing like some toxic, bottom-dwelling ocean creature who lies motionless in the sediment for hours only to explode and seize any smaller creature unlucky enough to swim within reach." This is writerly prose that makes us see, really see.

Beyond that, what we feel, in Jay's fiction, along with the emotions that grip and move the characters themselves, is a certain freedom, the willingness of the novelist to let things move in and out of pointed relevance, to guide the narrative with a total command of its direction and momentum but with a corresponding sense that it can afford to indulge its curiosity this way and that without fearing a fatal or even temporary loss of significant control. There is method in Jay's fiction, and structure, but not, we feel, compulsion. He has given us a well-made fiction that breathes and allows us, as readers, to breathe. And for that, as for much else, both edification and pleasure, we look ahead to further works by this gifted writer.

ANNE MICHAELS [2000]

"It's no metaphor to feel the influence of the dead in the world," we read in Anne Michaels' novel, *Fugitive Pieces*, and though we may wish to resist the literalness of that insistence, we feel the influence of the dead quite as much as Anne could wish as we make our way through her novel. "When the prisoners were forced to dig up the mass graves," we read, "the dead entered them through their pores and were carried through their bloodstreams to their brains and hearts. And through their blood into another generation. Their arms were into death up to the elbows, but not only into death—into music, into a memory of the way a husband or son leaned over his dinner, a wife's expression as she watched her child in the bath." The single, initiating image, the digging up of the mass graves, is continuously haunting, of course, so that finally, by paragraph's end, when "lost lives" make "molecular passage" into the hands of diggers, an emblem of transmutation has been irresistibly conveyed to us.

Yet it is not the passage alone that haunts us and impresses upon us its indelible authority. Anne's novel takes us over like a complex piece of music in which the rich sonorities multiply and interface so persistently that we are steadily engulfed. Cristina Garcia rightly refers to "the light-web" of Anne's language, which alternately illuminates and obscures, so that—quite as Anne herself has it at one point in her novel—memories "overtake us like a shadow," and "a truth appears suddenly in the middle of a thought, a hair on a lens."

Yet one would not wish to suggest that the fine, measured radiance of Anne's prose is all, or the patient conjuring and playing out of memories, or the ethical fortitude. There is, occasionally, something hard and unforgiving in the several perspectives Anne unfolds. Wounds are uncovered, failures of love or concern sharply anatomized. What Anne calls "the absolute, inviolate necessity of pleasure" is sharply conveyed. The primary drama of loss and mourning yields now and then to the search for fact or sensation. Anne's sustained inquiry into the effects of war and atrocity can seem, now and again, a study of "the random precision" of evil, so that fact and cause can open suddenly into the uncanny, even the whimsical. "The tornado prowls the street," Anne writes at one point; "it seems to stroll leisurely, selecting its victims, capricious, the sinister black funnel slithering across the landscape, whining with the sound of a thousand trains."

In such passages, as throughout Anne's novel, one is moved to remark the poet's command of image and detail; to say, with others, how much a poet's novel is *Fugitive Pieces*, that its author was of course a poet before she became, made herself, a novelist. But this is also at least a bit misleading. For Anne is, in *Fugitive Pieces*, altogether a novelist, though with a poet's command of resources not always thought essential to writers of fiction. The narrative momentum never fails, in spite of the intricate, discontinuous construction of the several narrative threads, and the enigmatic transparency of the action is consistently satisfying.

Just so, one wants to note that Anne's poetry, collected in several award-winning volumes, was never a warm-up for *Fugitive Pieces*, and stands in its own right as a central aspect of her achievement.

LEONARD MICHAELS [1994]

Reading Leonard Michaels has been compared to taking a number of hard blows to the head and groin. And in fact, that seems about right. In his stories and journals and novellas Lenny has found a powerful and bruising way to talk about very painful, sometimes frightening and humiliating things. His characters are frequently obsessives, haunted by thoughts of sex and violence and betrayal. Often they are haunted as well by the ghosts of Freud, Marx, Nietzsche and Kafka. The prose alternates between the stacatto and the lyric, the grimly blunt and the absurd. An aura of depravity and trauma is evoked without apology or elaborate explanation. With every sentence we feel we are under the spell of a driven, manic force, and often when we are about to cry out our wonder we're not sure whether it's a call of distress or a shout of anxious laughter to which we're driven. Though Lenny's work at its best administers a terrific beating, it is always in the service of a vision intense and capacious, and—as others have rightly said—it can break your heart and make you laugh.

In a recent work Lenny tells us he had "an early notion of guilt as fundamental to life," that "a strange mechanism of feelings drew me away from simple happiness into inward complications, like one who is depressed by holidays." This disposition seems mostly true of the characters in Lenny's fiction as well. They hunger for meaning even when they are most reckless and find themselves in the grip of one or another delirium. They wish often to be better than they are, to get free of delirium, but they move irrevocably in an air of feverish or lost connections and find themselves mocking—albeit with the taste of something bitter in their throats—the very idea of advancing, as Lenny puts it,

186

"to a higher level of thought" or feeling. In fact, Lenny's work expresses a loathing for most varieties of refinement, which he associates with dullness, good taste and the denial of elementary emotions. "I'd heard people say," he once wrote, "that the Nazis had undermined western civilization, and brought meaning itself into question. If so, I hadn't noticed. Too big; an idea like the sky; too vague. Western civilization was a course in universities, a hypothetical construction invented by Professors. Grief and rage were real."

There are, of course, in this remarkable little passage from what is an "occasional" personal essay, several accents, unmistakable emphases, like the words "invented by Professors," a formulation nicely identifying what has always seemed to Lenny a deep flaw, a basic falsity in American—one hesitates to say western—intellectual life. And there is, by contrast, the preference—it is a preference—for grief and rage, emotions inevitably true, which is to say, reliable, belonging to all of us, common, available, though more than occasionally denied.

But we note as well, in so brief a passage, other characteristic features of Lenny's writing, the surprising figure of speech—"an idea like the sky"—, a casual, biting sarcasm—"I hadn't noticed"—, the adoption of resonant expressions—"undermined western civilization"—which the reader trained by Lenny's prose will know at once to resist and to read with the requisite irony. The wonder of it is, of course, that at bottom Lenny is an earnest writer, with an obvious and deep feeling for ideas and something like a reverence for selected thinkers and writers. He is, in his fiction and in his essays, responsive not only to grief and rage but to the softer emotions, though tenderness is not the word that comes most readily to mind when you think of Lenny's work. In the end, what makes him so bruising a writer is the sense he conveys of writing out of an obstructed intelligence ever wrestling with a welter of inchoate emotions too powerful to be fully mastered. That communicated sense is at the root of the difficult satisfaction we take in his brilliant, abrasive work.

Lenny's books of course include the short novel *The Men's Club* and three brilliant collections: *Going Places, I Would Have Saved Them If I Could,* and *Shuffle.* I'd say more about these books if Lenny didn't loathe long introductions—as he's told me more than once.

STEVEN MILLHAUSER [1995]

Steven Millhauser is an authentic American original: so one feels at once as one reads novels like *Edwin Mullhouse* or the brilliant stories collected in *The Penny Arcade* or *The Barnum Museum*. So one hears from writers so diverse as Russell Banks and Robert Pinsky, Irving Howe and Bharati Mukherjee. But though, in speaking with confident enthusiasm of Steve's originality, we know just what we mean, it is misleading to assimilate his work to the post-modern tradition in which he principally operates.

In fact, one compares Steve with Borges or Calvino or Nabokov only because one is utterly reluctant to compare him to anyone else. His aesthetic control and meticulous intelligence are often—and rightfully—remarked, but there are more important aspects of his work that set him apart from his predecessors. A fantasist with a taste for the gratuitous and farcical, he is also a strangely sober, sometimes melancholic writer. Within a single sentence he often moves from inspired whimsy and invention to disillusionment. For all of his commitment to creating an air of legend, as he puts it, the better to set off creatures perfect and complete in themselves, he is ever alert to the fact that "today's novelty is tomorrow's ennui," the marvelous "a revelation that never comes."

In a way, then, it is tempting to think of Steve as the most balanced and mature of writers, however much he is absorbed in the world of fantasy, sheer play, and childhood. The balance has to do with the equilibrium in Steve's work between abandon and constraint, innocence and irony, exhilaration and defeat. Reluctant to let go of childhood—or at least of its prerogatives—the fiction steadily undermines its own playfulness and intimates all that childhood, like art, cannot sustain. If, often, Steve trades in the eccentric or bizarre—one thinks of the erotic miniatures sometimes painted upon the sides and tips of the nipples of court ladies in the story "Cathay"—he never seems far from dis-enchantment. Even his language is suffused with these alterna-tions and ambivalences. Pregnant, even lugubrious passages are undercut or brushed by the ironically academic, the finicky, the fantastically observant. This, one feels throughout, is a writer of extraordinary versatility, who knows precisely what language and invention can and cannot accomplish. But unlike other gifted "lie-minded men"—I take that expression from William Gass—Steve is also, always, offering us what feels like the full richness of life. It may not be—often it isn't—the life we live, but it is in every sense a philosophically and emotionally adequate world.

STEVEN MILLHAUSER [1996]

The first and possibly the most important thing to say about the work of Steven Millhauser is that it is a pleasure to read. We say *pleasure* and think *pleasure* because pleasure is not always thought to be an important feature of our response to the literature we admire. Pleasure is, of course, a relative term, suggesting greater and lesser intensities, but with Steven Millhauser we have no need to settle for the one kind at the expense of the other. His fictions, long and short, provide the lesser intensities of symmetry, precision, modesty and proportion, but they also provide surprise, abundance of detail, tonal richness, and human feeling—feeling: as in melancholy, longing, envy, ennui, disappointment and—occasionally—exhilaration. These greater intensities no reader of Millhauser is apt to miss, and no good reader will fail to appreciate the others.

A particular kind of pleasure, much favored by contemporary literary academics—or so they say—is associated with the word indeterminacy. This pleasure Millhauser also provides, if by "indeterminacy" we mean, simply, that a Millhauser fiction is usually of many minds about a number of different things and resists, utterly, the reduction of its vital substance to a meaning or a formula. But Millhauser has little in common with a species of writer for whom indeterminacy is a mode of condescension, a way of willfully obscuring what is obvious or substituting cleverness for a full commitment to the materials at hand. We take pleasure in Millhauser's indeterminacies because they are not a form of one-upsmanship, because they help us to grasp the essential playfulness and venturesomeness of his imagination.

Millhauser is, as has often been said, a fantasist. He has,

no doubt about it, a taste for the whimsical and the farcical, for hyperbole and childhood. But there is nothing frivolous in his version of the fantastic, so that even his most outlandish contrivances are invested with an essential earnestness and purpose. We may not, as readers, always feel the presence of an urgent, glittering eye, holding us fiercely to the page, but we hear, on every page of Millhauser, the accent of the fabulist for whom this is the story I must tell, and this is the story they must hear. At times, revelation is at stake; elsewhere, something less, but never less than the story-teller's conviction that the work is a way of igniting the imagination, rescuing daydream from irrelevance, idea from ponderousness.

Millhauser's works together offer us something like a world, a world in which certain kinds of dreaming and thinking are possible, others not. But it is a world, also, with unpredictable features. Child's play yields, now and again, to erotic mania, a world elsewhere suddenly looks more like—*mirabile dictu*—central Europe or Manhattan, and the topography of nineteenth century Hudson River communities is conflated with the contours of post-World War II small-town America. The world of the comic strip or the faux art catalogue exists side by side with the world of the middle-class family.

So, too, Millhauser's language moves between abandon and constraint, innocence and irony. Pregnant, even lugubrious passages are undercut by the dryly academic put-on, the finicky, the fanatically observant detail. Ingenuity is matched, at every point, by an uncommon ease and lack of pretension, an expression surprisingly direct, however punctuated by bright images and occasional eruptions of self-parody and mock satire. As one recent critic, writing in the *Washington Post*, nicely put it, Millhauser's actual sentences, however intricate and various, can rise "to a prose of such measured serenity and assurance that God himself might envy it."

Well, we who love Steven Millhauser's work do not envy him his prose or his genius. We are content simply to pass some considerable time in the company of his imagination, to celebrate the appearance of new work—his new novel is entitled *Martin Dressler*—, and to dip, again and yet again, into the restorative waters of the earlier books that have meant so much to us.

RICK MOODY [2000]

Though he is not yet forty years old, Rick Moody is one of the most admired writers in the country. He says that John Cheever is a hero, that they were once "similar topologically," but Rick's sentences do not at all resemble Cheever's, and so that so-called resemblance does not at all explain why Rick is admired. Others say he "dazzles with the sheer energy and near-reckless-ness he brings to his writing," but surely energy and recklessness do not in themselves an ever-expanding reputation make. No doubt many readers have been moved by Rick's early, relentless anatomization of the suburban, wasp upper middle-classes, a sector of the population for which many of us continue to hold a scarcely concealed contempt, as if persons traveling into Manhattan on commuter railroads five days each week and participating in key parties were somehow responsible for everything unsatisfactory in contemporary life. But other writers much less admired than Rick Moody have turned a satiric eye on those same wasp classes and showered upon the suburban elite a contempt guaranteed to win the gratitude of readers.

In fact, it is probably best, in approaching the work of Rick Moody, to dispense with all thought of John Cheever, or commuter suburbs "from hell," or the mordancies of late afternoon cocktails and early-evening bouts with drugs or extra-marital sex. The slide into depression and ennui has its compelling features in Rick's hands, but we begin to get at his distinctive strength only when we let his sentences rattle around in our heads and roll across our tongues. And those sentences, I'd suggest, are best scanned and studied and savored in a magnificent novel called *Purple America*. Rick's earlier novels had seemed accomplished and assured and knowing. Readers of *The Ice Storm* understood perfectly why—as one reviewer had it—"the numbing orthodoxy of New Canaan [Connecticut] would send anyone into sexual ferment" and "drugged-up" cynicism. But with *Purple America* we see the arrival of a writer with larger ambitions. The sentences are often long and sinuous, the syntax sometimes perilously fractured, the idiom unabashedly ripe or lyrical, the use of italics copious and audacious, here signalling stammered thoughts, there emphasizing what one writer calls "the alienating public languages of the modern age, of technology, of corporate-speak, of nuclear-industry euphemism." We move steadily through a screen of intersecting idioms in *Purple America*, and though the public languages do in fact feel impoverishing and alienating and more than a little sinister, they are continually offset by alternate languages, from the language of motherhood to the language of kisses, from almost unbuttoned lyricism to the "faint and inscrutable," as Rick puts it.

Yet never in this work, or in Rick's other novels, does the writing seem merely performative or preening. Though Rick is in no way averse to theatricality or eloquence, his reader is absorbed, as novel readers tend to be, in the drama of character and class, culture and consciousness. We attend, as we must, to the continuous tunings and adjustments in language, to the way people think and speak, but we are never less than interested in them, in their susceptibility to tenderness or rage, their sometimes arbitrary, almost motiveless eruptions of sentiment or revulsion, their evolving sense of how things going on around them out there affect their loyalties and their prospects. No one would think to describe Rick as a topical writer with a primary commitment to theme or subject. But his fiction engages the world as if it were possible to derive from that process something like a coherent vision. And if something less than a perfect coherence is achieved, that seems to us all to the good, a mark of Rick's resistance to conventional closure. For all of his unarguable virtuosity, there is something a bit raw in the rush of Rick's writing, like a wind capable of lashing—quite as Wallace Stevens once said—"everything at once," so that our ongoing impression is of a landscape, a mindscape, suffused by "lightning and the thickest thunder."

RICK MOODY [2001]

Rick Moody, like most of our best fiction writers, defies summary description. His works are various, his purposes unpredictable. There is, to be sure, a certain kind of sentence, even a sentence-sequence, that has Moody written all over it, but the manner is but one of his distinctive attributes. By manner we mean, in this case, a gift for effects, an ear and predilection for strong cadences, rhetorical flourishes, highly colored language, peculiar shifts in diction and tone and syntax. Not that there is but a single manner in Rick's work, though there is an unmistakable accent belonging to him and to him alone. The accent is more frequently found in the stories than in the novels, though it appears in its most expansive and powerful form in the novel *Purple America*, where the long hovering sentences, threatening to whirl and spiral out of control, bursting with plenitudes, are the motor of a book that seems to me one of the most audacious and sustained novels by an American writer in the last twenty-five years.

You can hear the accent almost anywhere in the stories, even when there are no long sentences. Listen, please, to the following: "This one's about the stuff that Lucy said. Lucy, a woman I knew once. Lucy who took seventy hits of acid in one day and, in a way, lived to tell. She'd been living in a squat in Burlington, Vermont, when she did it. Living like a runaway. The source of the drugs is unimportant. They were available. Lucy took the poison and meandered along the streets, meandering until it kicked in, until its contingency was her contingency." We note, in this fragment, the obvious, which includes the casual and pointed repetitions of ordinary or important words, including the name

Lucy, the word *living*, and variants of the word *meandered*. We note as well the sudden shift in diction, from the colloquial to the suddenly elevated, as from *stuff* and *squat* and *kicked in* to the sentence-finisher, "until its contingency was her contingency." There is a good deal of that sort of shifting in Rick's prose, swerves that serve not only to emphasize particular words but to unsettle the reader, complicate his sense of where exactly the narrative is coming from and what is its dominant tone—detached? scholarly? mischievous? hip and emotionally invested at the same time? Often in Rick's work the farcical is not far removed from the tender and concerned. Irony and special effects are employed deliberately in works whose manifest purpose seems anything but sheer performative overdrive employed mainly for its own pretty or thrilling sake. Even in the passage quoted a moment ago, where you can tell that more of the same emphasis on rhetorical effects is just ahead, as indeed it is, it is, you are alerted to the impending development of the human material, which, for this writer, is more than raw material, more than the occasion it presents for display and excess.

The effects in Rick's work include a variety of cerebral features, conceptual terms and philosophical riffs, such as one might associate with the persistent use of a term like contingency. Just so, Rick's fondness for inviting the reader into the writer's compositional process is more than generosity and more than mischief. When in the story called "Phrase Book," he peppers the exposition with the word "maybe" and with "whichever way you looked at it," you know that he is, alright, having a good time for himself, but also seriously working out his thoughts and feelings. Sure, he openly announces that his character's "past was mine to derive," and several times he mischievously revises the contructed scenario of her past. Sure, he now and again catches himself running on too rapidly with the headlong narrative , and will sometimes interrupt himself with a "Wait, let me go back a bit" or something like that. But our sense throughout is that Rick really wants to know what is at issue in the life he is evoking. He is really, seriously inquiring into the possibility that a life will assume a certain shape and momentum without the standard assortment of motives or causes. Perhaps, as he suggests, the story he is constructing has to allow for "all these possibilities in solution," because all of them exist in the character's own memory, her own dim, fragmented sense of where and who and what she is.

All of which is to say that Rick Moody is a writer with a fearless writerly disposition, a writer willing to use anything he can come up with to accomplish his ends, which include nothing less than the ends to which first-rate fiction aspires, ends which include the probing of the human heart and, yes, the continuous engagement with the world's central mysteries. Yes, the epithets typically employed to characterize this writer—inventive, wicked, nightmarish, unnerving, and exhilarating—are more or less apt, and there's no need to pretend that in truth Rick wants simply to tell a good story or to move us to pity and fear and empathy. But yes, Rick Moody is a writer both moving and intellectually ambitious and he does call to mind, continually, the great, larger aims of the very best writers, in whose company he surely belongs.

BHARATI MUKHERJEE [1999]

For twenty-five years now, Bharati Mukherjee has helped to transform the way we think about the American experiment. In a range of novels, stories, and memoirs she has explored the meaning of immigration, displacement, and otherness and has taught us how to think about the collision of cultures and identities. No other contemporary writer has had so many fresh things to tell us about the American newness, and no other has demonstrated so cunning a combination of what Margaret Atwood once called the "unforgiving" and the "elegiac." Bharati, quite as Atwood contends, has never been one to "let anyone off the hook," and one counts on her to write about—in everything she examines—all things "unsavory," which is to say, precisely what "the natives would prefer to sweep under the carpet."

About what has Bharati been unforgiving? Why, no more than the usual things most of us do our best to forget: the brutalities—large and small—of the powerful, the many languages of deceit, the instigations to ethnic strife, the image-panderings of the well-meaning, the use of victim status as a substitute for ambition and the will to change. Bharati has always seen to the very heart of such matters, and it is therefore not at all surprising that, now and then, her writing should strike an elegiac note, briefly remembering what has been lost, or what one thought one had before one saw—everything.

Other writers, of course, have also come to us in the posture of the disabused, the clear-eyed and unforgiving. But one has never felt in the writing of Bharati Mukherjee the rancor, the instinct to even old scores that we have come to associate with the injured and oppressed in our culture. Probably this has much to do with a steadiness of purpose, an essential sanity, and a capacity for hope in Bharati's writing. For all that she sees and sets before us, for all that stirs and angers and disgusts, there is in her work a saving wit and an absorption in the actual that restrains the instinct to caricature or pillory. Bharati's is a dark, sometimes harsh vision, but it comes through to us with so much of the taste and color of ordinariness clinging to it that we believe in it and discover in it openings for sympathy.

Bharati's first novels, *Wife* and *The Tiger's Daughter*, were quietly eloquent forays into the territory that she has steadily made her own. Otherness in these works was at once a condition of suffering and of not-knowing, and it was evoked with an utterly sober clarity, by turns satiric and charitable. But the trauma of otherness took on additional weight and complication with the publication of *Days and Nights in Calcutta*, a non-fiction book Bharati wrote with Clark Blaise. There, in alternating views of an India re-claimed and discovered, Bharati seemed to learn that she was no longer an expatriate, but that she had become, somehow, what she has since called an unhyphenated American fiercely committed to creating for herself and others a new American identity.

The fierceness is frequently discernible in the extraordinary volumes of stories that followed—in the book *Darkness*, published in 1985, and in *The Middleman*, which won the National Book Critics Circle Award in 1988. In these stories, and in later novels like *Jasmine* and *The Holder of the World*, Bharati extends her inquiry into displacement and identity, confronting her readers with many strains of newness, but without the phony exoticism or the fantasies of purifying violence that often distort or cheapen our view of the other. In Bharati, violence cuts and hurts; the exotic is a token of lost mastery; the exploited and humiliated are recognizably human though sometimes grossly unappealing; the unmasking of stereotypes and contradictions often gives little satisfaction, though it ever seems necessary and bracing.

In their candor, color, and sheer narrative drive, the fictions of Bharati Mukherjee have no equal in the literature of immigration and displacement.

BHARATI MUKHERJEE [2001]

In the introduction to her 1985 short-story collection, *Darkness*, Bharati Mukherjee writes: " I see my 'immigrant' story replicated in a dozen American cities, and instead of seeing my Indianness as a fragile identity to be preserved against obliteration (or worse, a 'visible' disfigurement to be hidden), I see it now as a set of fluid identities to be celebrated." The robustness of that statement is discernible in much that Bharati has written in the last twenty-five years or so. Often in her writing we see embodiments of the fluid identities liberated in the American new world. Often in her work characters are surprised to find they have the words to speak to an alien other. The discovery of a common language, a way to get around ostensibly immutable divisions of class and ethnicity, is more than occasionally at issue in novels designed, apparently, to "deconstruct," as one of Bharati's characters says in *The Holder of the World*, "the barriers of time and geography."

But, sad or happy to say, celebration is not the word that comes chiefly to mind as we engage the writing of Bharati Mukherjee. This process of deconstructing barriers is no picnic, apparently, and the faculties enlisted in the service of understanding are frequently mobilized for purposes not precisely enlightened or edifying. Bharati's fiction is often, most often, dark and tumultuous. The energies and motives that move her characters are often predatory, rapacious. Fluidity in the realm of identity is apt, most of the time, surely in Bharati's fiction, to look like characterless drift or what may well be called "multiple personality disorder." The celebration of diversity turns more than a little bit scary when the diversity exists in an unstable person whose m.o. is the putting on of masks whose only purpose is to control, and manipulate, multiply deceived others. So much for the celebration of fluidity, then, in the fiction of a writer with a preternaturally good nose for treachery and the courage to examine the deceptions associated with identity politics.

The most brilliant and lacerating of Bharati's recent novels is a book called *Leave it to Me*, built around a young identity-seeker, who eventually lands in the California Bay Area, there to become " a kind of outlaw, on the side of other outlaws," a fellow-travelling companion of the wretched of the earth. There is nothing remotely comforting about the descent of the young woman in this novel, and Bharati is scathingly satiric about the inane pieties of our culture, especially when the inanities are served up in the name of psychic freedom and limitless potential. But she is no less scathing about the purely credulous, those who are oblivious about what is being done to them.

Bharati has long been a muscular writer, never glib, never precious, never eager to press into service a literary word when a more familiar word would do as well. The color in her writing comes, at least in part, from the extraordinary diversity of persons, costumes, places, objects she handles. With her customary materials so frequently exotic and requiring, therefore, full, even lavish evocation, she needs to maintain a wary resistance to excessive coloring effects, superfluities of description or ornamentation or mood-tones. We feel, in Bharati's hands, no frivolous "touches," no worked up poignancies. All is consummately well ordered, the alternating moods elegiac or punishing, sympathetic or bemused. The controlling intelligence at works seems to us at once authoritative and inquisitive, its full absorption in what it wishes to examine so thorough as to restrain any instinct to caricature or pillory, though satire, as intimated earlier, is very much a part of Bharati's characteristic repertoire. The exploited and the humiliated in Bharati's work are always recognizably human, though sometimes unappealing, as distasteful, in fact, as the powerful, as the operators and multi-national corporate managers and small-time predators whose habits of expropriation and terror she seems to us to understand as well as any writer we have.

Clearly, then, the fictions of Bharati Mukherjee give us access to a world and to a diverse set of preoccupations we find continuously compelling. She is our great writer of immigration and displacement, and she has helped to create an understanding of the American empire greatly more capacious and credible than anything we had before she came upon the literary scene.

CHARLES NEWMAN [1999]

Say the name Charles Newman and you think imme-
diately *avant garde, post-modern, black comedy*. From the earliest
stages of his career as a novelist and story writer, Charles has
negotiated the far edge of every fictional genre and formal convention. He has been by turns oblique and confiding, allusive and
prophetic, prankish and vatic. He has told engaging stories and
done everything in his considerable power to make those very
stories seem somehow almost incidental to the range of his other
interests—in ideas, in power and money, in linguistic play, in the
uses of irony, in metaphor. Often described as a writer's writer,
a poet-philosopher, a man infatuated with language for its own
sake, Charles is certainly no one's idea of a straightforward realist,
but he has created a wide range of vivid characters and exhib-
ited a relentless fascination with the history and culture of this
century. His fiction early inspired writers like Joyce Carol Oates,
William Gass and John Gardner to speak of him as the creator of
artworks "without genre."

Of course just about anyone who was interested in art and
fiction in the mid-1980's read Charles's stirring, much debated,
much disputed, often scorned, often loved polemical work, *The
Post-Modern Aura*. And what was clear in that brilliant, extravagant book was Charles's uncertainty about a great many things,
including the prospects for success in the very medium he had
chosen to work in himself. Why, he wanted to know, did post-
modern writing so often disappoint, vex, irritate? Why was it too
often pretentious and empty and posturing? There is a sense in
which Charles's book answers these questions, or recommends
ways to think about them, but in the main his book raises more

questions than it answers, and provokes and teases and confounds and delights more than it instructs. Though, like all of Charles's work, it is informed by enormous learning, speculative abandon and what used to be called "an experience of the world," it is also informed, like his fiction, by the imp of the perverse. And like all of his work, *The Post-Modern Aura* succeeds most assuredly and memorably in saying *no* to the devaluation of art and literature in late twentieth century America.

But nothing I've said should suggest that Charles—whatever his occasional polemical instincts—is anything less than a true fictionist, a fabulator, who knows always how to keep the action going and to resist the essayism that often obstructs the narrative energy of otherwise impressive works by comparably learned writers. The sheer brio and charge of Charles's writing, the quality that moved the novelist Paul West years ago to describe one of his books as "a book like a shark with a loop in its womb," are very much on display in the first volume of a trilogy he has been working at for many years, from which he will read a bit tonight. For me the most impressive thing by far in this work, which will be published, I believe, some time in the not distant future, is Charles's mastery of a central European cast of mind which is at once familiar, plausible, and largely invented. This mastery cannot be conveyed in selective quotations, but it is everywhere apparent in the texture of the novel, in its idioms, its psychological oddities, its combined lustre and dimness, its recourse to history, its melancholia and sometimes enforced gaiety. In these many qualities we hear the echoes of a great many voices—of Kafka and Kis, of Robert Musil and Gregor Von Rezzori most especially, I would say. And though we feel, as well, the presence of voices from another world, the drive and manic plotting we associate with Pynchon and Barth and other American post-modern writers, the Eastern European sensibility remains ever dominant here, the accent unmistakable and alluring. I know of no other novel so accomplished in its command of this accent.

How does Newman's handling of his material compare with Musil's? There is more extremity and play in Newman, more cleverness and not so very much sobriety. While Musil turned only reluctantly to narrative, and was more entirely committed to essayism, even in his fiction, Newman has the greater instinct for narrative, never allows his action to bog down in tracts which function, as in Musil, as illustrations of abstract ideas. Newman knows the difference between embodiment and exemplification, and understands that only the one is the proper province of the novel.

In short, Charles Newman is that rare, wonderful thing, a writer of convulsively original and beautiful books, and I am delighted to introduce him.

HOWARD NORMAN [2001]

Tonight marks the first of what I hope will be many readings at the Writers Institute by Howard Norman. He is, I find, an extraordinary writer whose peculiar strengths and affinities seem somewhat clear to us the moment we set his work alongside the work of other, very different writers. For some reason John Updike comes immediately to mind. Why? Perhaps because no one could be more different. Read any one of Howard Norman's novels, *The Northern Lights*, or *The Bird Artist*, or *The Museum Guard*, and you know that in these fictional climates you find little or none of the insistent sensuality, the self-conscious lyricism, the sometimes complacent aestheticism that we associate, for better or worse, with the prose of John Updike, who has been described as an "acolyte of plenitude."

By contrast, Howard Norman is a master of absences, reductions, diminishments. He seems most comfortable with, most persistently drawn to the forsaken, the provincial, the muted, the defeated. Where Updike lavishes and adds, Howard Norman withholds, not coyly, but out of respect for the greyness, the austerity, the marginality of the lives he mostly studies. Where Updike cannot, it seems, resist the temptation to embroider a sentence, swell a metaphor, Howard is more circumspect and self-effacing in his relation to language, willing to believe, and to act upon the belief, that in fiction as in poetry, less can be more, effects won by a sparing use of metaphor and adverb and textural brocade.

This is in no way to suggest that Howard Norman's prose is artificially severe, or pinched, a writing resolutely or perpetually at degree zero. Far from it. But you have only to examine a passage of description in a novel like *The Museum Guard* to note how entirely the opportunity to embroider has been resisted. Details frequently abound, so that a bedroom has not just wallpaper but "flower-print wallpaper." The trunk by the bed is both "padlocked" and "wooden." But even the detail is sparse, withholding, for we do not feel that it is meant to reveal very much or to carry with it an emotional charge. Nor does it at all bring to mind the author's impressive resources of language, his compulsive addictions to particular colorings or rhetorical devices. The hallmark of his writing is sufficiency, plain-talk, an unostentatious mastery of an idiom perfectly tuned to capture the thoughts and exchanges of persons without any special gifts of language or intellect, people who may, sometimes, be aware of their smallness or provinciality of outlook and expression but whose awareness would only be expressible in the most meagre and unliterary of idioms.

The remarkable thing, in this body of work so largely devoid of flamboyance and authorial self-importance, is that it is, as many, many others have noted, often thrilling and resonant. Plain language in Howard Norman often conveys with astonishing force and exactitude varieties of idiosyncratic thought and behavior that go beyond mere commonplace, harmless eccentricity. A grey steadiness of perspective can reveal, in this work, disquieting abrasions and obsessions. The tranquil and mundane sometimes erupts, the apparently colorless, serviceable idiom of an apparently bland first-person narrator suddenly a vehicle for transporting us to places in the soul we had not thought to visit. What one reader has referred to as the alternation in Howard's writing from "ground-level" to "aerial sightings" creates in us an odd, mixed sensation, as of witnesses mired in an all-too real, grimly oppressive reality, and on the other hand, of witnesses observing, transfixed, the unfolding of a dark fable too obscure for us to understand completely, whatever the attendant narrative compulsion to explain and conclude.

Howard Norman is a writer of singular, uncanny gifts whose power to move us and engage us seems often not to stem from the rhetorical deployments we associate with work so enthralling. He is also a writer whose work demonstrates, in a compelling way, the revelatory and humanizing power of fiction.

JOYCE CAROL OATES [2000]

We are gathered this evening, as in many previous summer evenings at the Writers Institute, to listen in on another installment of the work of Joyce Carol Oates. To say that she is one of our best writers is by now as obvious as to say that her energies are fabulous, her imagination protean. When, last summer, one of our own institute visitors, himself a distinguished man of letters, quietly mentioned at dinner that of course Joyce was one of the most interesting essayists in the country, the rest of us at the table could only nod our heads in agreement and come out with some version of the words "but that doesn't begin to get at what is most compelling in her work."

You might instead begin by saying that, if you wanted in some distant future to offer to someone from another country, or another planet, some sense of what this country has been like in the second half of the twentieth century, you might well recommend that the visitor read six or seven novels and, say, forty or fifty stories by Joyce Carol Oates. Those would provide some fair measure of our common restlessness and our susceptibility to disillusion or self-pity, of our fanaticisms and our earnestness, our vitality and our innocence. It seems sometimes that Joyce's fictions are set on the ragged edge of the universe, though in many obvious ways they are as earth-bound and as fully situated as any novels we know. Characters move frequently on the margins of sanity, obsessed, driven, alert to the prospect of chaos and disorder, though alert also to the lure of something less menacing, more familiar, which, often, they have not the words or the will to summon.

Now and again the characters in Joyce's fiction are moved

not only to live and relive their fates but to reflect, to suppose that it is possible to take control of their lives by naming what has had its way with them. They think "evil" or "soul," formulate resolutions, talk to themselves or their lovers about desire and longing, invoke what they call "perennial questions." But even in such works, where characters are articulate and educated, where there is some capacity for detachment and stock-taking, the rush of the narrative is generally headlong, even frantic. Crisis is in the air the characters breathe, and even the modest, sensitive souls are flung forward by desire or by the sheer force of events whose underlying configurations are frequently inaccessible to them. The ruptured syntax of Joyce's sentences will often convey dis-orientation or panic, the abrupt motions and reversals of minds caught up in something over-mastering, dimly outlined but, to them, palpable, inescapable.

Even modest lives without overt histrionic dimension are opened up in Joyce's fiction so that their susceptibility to unravel-ing rages or seizures of compensatory violence becomes essential to our sense of them and weighs more and more heavily on their sense of themselves. Those, readers, who typically resist the con-nection between erotic possession and violence, between resent-ment or envy and love, are shaken by Joyce's fiction, shaken by its sinister embodiment of surrender. Stop, you want often to say to Joyce's characters. Don't go there. Take a deeper breath, look the other way. But the currents of feeling set loose are too much for the characters, and rapidly seem too powerful to al-low for beneficent intervention or well-meaning, admonitory, readerly wishful thinking. We feel ourselves over-mastered, sus-ceptible, diminished.

And yet we are grateful for this ever-developing sensation. We register the shocks of descent or disorientation as aspects of what one writer calls a "scouring honesty" in Joyce's work. Joyce is a true subversive, for whom enlightenment is at once seductive and unreliable. We feel in her work the powers of love and hope, but these seem to us, are made to seem, corruptible, their promise rapidly clouded. Nowhere in Joyce's work is this process of destabilization more powerfully evoked than in her recent novel *Blonde*, about which much has already been written. But it may be useful, in closing, simply to note that with this novel, Joyce has not only anatomized the psyche of an extraordinarily vivid character, here based on Marilyn Monroe, and offered us a compelling vision of American society in the middle of the century just ended, but has re-made an entire literary genre, forcing us to consider anew what are the vital possibilities of biographical or historical fiction at the present moment. The fact that Joyce has done no less with other genre forms, from the gothic thriller to the romance novel, from the political novel to the family chronicle, makes her achievement in the new work all the more remarkable.

JOYCE CAROL OATES [2001]

A few years ago there appeared an essay by Joyce Carol Oates entitled "The Aesthetics of Fear." It begins with the question, "Why should we wish to experience fear?" The essay takes us through a whole variety of literary works, from *The Odyssey* to *King Lear*, from Ovid's *Metamorphoses* to Bram Stoker's *Dracula*, positing in a number of ways the central question, "Why do we wish as a species to approach the unspeakable, the unknowable, the vision that, like Medusa with her horrific head of serpents, will prove unbearable?" And though it is unfair and impossible to summarize a literary essay so subtle and cunning and rich, I will say that Joyce's essay concludes by suggesting that what we fear most "is not death" but "the loss of meaning and, more especially, the very thought that the species"—we ourselves—"may become extinct in our complicity with the predator—the cannibal/vampire—within."

Thinking about Joyce's work, as I often do, and not simply in July when I prepare to introduce her on her annual visit to the Summer Writers Institute, I often confront the centrality in her fiction of the aesthetics of fear. This dimension of the work is most obvious in her gothic stories and novels, where the trappings of terror and blood, the perverse and the sacrificial, are impossible to overlook. But in no other major writer does fear almost invariably play so large a role as it does in the works of Joyce Oates. The occasions of fear are various in these works, of course, as various as the motives and stratagems of victims and perpetrators, the merely anxious and the actually abused or violated. Often the fear evoked is in the nature of a free-floating, indefinable dread, elsewhere a fear related to a substantial threat or explosive circumstance. But at bottom, it would seem, what Joyce calls the loss of meaning is very much at issue, and the fear most real to us as readers is a fear associated as much with the dissolution or betrayal of the self as with any external brutality or violence. Joyce's word, complicity, perfectly captures the specific quality of the fear most usually felt by her characters.

This fear is, much of the time, not at all what would seem usual for Joyce's people, who are often mature, ostensibly civilized persons, who read books, go to college, attend cocktail parties, make sophisticated noises, strive, aspire, regret and practice the usual varieties of forebearance. But there is, in Joyce's characters, what can only be called a susceptibility that makes them vulnerable—not merely to the sentiment of fear but to the loss of control that gives to fear its most plausible and primitive dimension. How often in Joyce's work does some small thing, something occasional or accidental, become the instigation for the release of emotions from which, we feel, no good can come. How often does a character find herself feeling what she would rather not feel, yield to a suggestion too incredible to be entertained, let alone embraced?

The brilliance of Joyce's fiction, the implacable authority it exercises over our emotions, has much to do with its ferocious concentration, its often breathless, gathering momentum, its distilling of fear to an oppressive essence in light of which rational alternatives seem irrelevant, paltry, evasive. What is most dreamlike in Joyce's work is the sense it conveys of entrapment, of some insidious germ working to undermine the stable structure of our lives. Joyce's fictional universe is replete with guilt and a whole range of intense if sometimes shadowy emotions, but it is not a realm in which fault plays any part. Fault belongs, after all, to a universe in which persons may be expected to exercise rational control in a degree largely absent from Joyce's characters, who are possessed by the fate assigned to them by their emotions, and who are real to us because they cannot but be what they are.

That Joyce succeeds so powerfully in making real to us what are sometimes extreme states of consciousness, distortions of ordinary experience, is of course a mark of her virtuosity in novels given over to serial killers and other "exceptional" figures. But much the same kind of virtuosity is at work in Joyce's bringing to life of so-called ordinary persons, whose fear of the darkness within them, whose susceptibility to emotions remote from their own sense of themselves, make them, at least intermittently, driven creatures with Joyce's peculiar, animating mark upon them. Joyce Carol Oates has given us an astounding succession of works, an entire created universe, vast with emotion and possibility, with balked desires and inexpressible intensities. The whisper, at times the scream of conspiracy is ever present in these works, and it is impossible to read them without feeling that we are uncomfortably complicit in much, or all, that is at stake. The truths to which Joyce's fiction points us are compelling and—as we can say only of our bravest writers—altogether bottomless.

MICHAEL ONDAATJE [1999]

When Michael Ondaatje first visited the Summer Writers Institute four years ago his work was not exactly a secret held in strictest confidence by the cognoscenti. The poets on our staff had long sung his praises, and novelists like William Kennedy and Russell Banks had declared Michael's Booker-Prize-winning novel, *The English Patient*, a beautiful and moving book. Many of those who came to Michael's reading here in 1995 had already read at least one of his books. And yet it seemed to me that Michael was still not widely read in this country, that he was regarded primarily as a maker of exquisite literary objects, someone to read slowly, by the relative handful of readers who have time and disposition to savor what is rare and beautiful.

Of course Michael is in fact a maker of exquisite literary objects, and of course he demands, he expects, of readers a quiet attentiveness that is generally in very short supply. But Michael has found his attentive readers, or created them, and he has brought them to him not with extravagant prestidigitations but with the writerly cunning and natural command of idiom and structure that are everywhere on display in his work. So much has Michael reached the widest imaginable audience for serious writing that it does truly seem almost superfluous to introduce him, to sing his praises, to remind his faithful readers of what he has done. So I apologize for what will likely seem superfluous.

From the first Michael was admired as a poet, and responses even to books like *In the Skin of a Lion*, books heavily invested in place and history, tended to stress Michael's lyricism and poetic roots. To be sure, Michael's prose writing often has about it the musical quality, the elegance and elusiveness we as-

218

sociate with the best poetry. But the register in Michael's fiction is not invariably lyric, and the narrative pulse is typically strong, the plotting intricate, however wayward Michael's compositional procedures. Political intrigue and reflection are at least informing elements. Issues are permitted, if only intermittently, to emerge and claim our attention. We are absorbed, moved, by the steady penetration of motive and the careful, suggestive outlining of individual psychology. The poetic features of Michael's novelistic fabric are but an aspect, albeit an essential aspect, of the enterprise.

Of course Michael has never stopped being a poet in the literal sense, that is, he has never stopped writing poems. His newest book, *Handwriting*, is a collection of lyrics set in Michael's first home, Sri Lanka, which is also the setting for his great memoir, *Running in the Family*. The poems in the new book are characteristically patient, measured, at once alert to violence and political turmoil and, at the same time, quiet, meditative, listening for silence. The poems often proceed by fragments, arresting insights succeeding closely observed, naked particulars. Anecdotes emerge fitfully, their torsos partially, largely cut off, obscured. Where there is something more than a torso, the unfolding narrative nonetheless seems often to conceal as much as it discloses. You feel, reading these poems, that you are entering a world you have never known before, learning its shapes and rhythms and obsessions and some of its historical resonances; but you feel, just as surely, that you are being initiated into mysteries you'll never quite know how to fathom or to articulate for anyone else. That is often the way it is with Michael's work, and the new poems do remind us of the continuities that have made of Michael's most recent fiction and poetry, however disparate in setting and substance, a coherent enterprise, always simultaneously bringing experience into brilliant, not quite fatal focus while seeing to it that much slips suggestively through our fingers like grains of sand, or, more precisely, like fine precious drops of holy water.

The poet Robert Creeley, attempting to get at, to name a quality as central to Michael's poetry as to his prose, and ill at ease, apparently, with "simple" mystery, asserts that the poems "read with the same whimsical precision and authority one finds in his prose." Nice, that poet's move to join "whimsical" with "precision," but wrong, in this case, not helpful, not precise, for "whimsical" is precisely what the poems are not, no more than the prose may reasonably be said to be. The authority, in fact, that Creeley rightly identifies with Michael's work emerges, at least in part, from its uncommon search for the inevitable, irreplaceable gesture and for what the poet Howard Nemerov once called "the exact, extortionate word." That the poems, like the prose, very occasionally permit a note of whimsy—say, in the juxtaposition of two apparently disparate incidents—in no way suggests a tendency in this work towards chance or vagrancy. The confident authority, the air of easy command that Michael's work exudes has everything to do with the utterly controlled surfaces of the writing, our sense that nothing could be—not for Michael, not for us—other than it is. The poems, like the prose, read with an uncanny, exacting precision, without which they would lack their unimpeachable authority.

MICHAEL ONDAATJE [2000]

A character in Michael Ondaatje's new novel, *Anil's Ghost*, set in Michael's native Sri Lanka at a time of violence and disorder, wonders at the marvelous skills of those who are adept at deciphering inscriptions. Elsewhere in the novel, almost everywhere, it seems, there is an emphasis on reading, interpreting signs, the search for precise markings, the charting of "possible trajectories." In situations of every kind people are given to making assessments, opening up geographies, inventing stories. The likely and the just-barely-possible seem almost equally seductive. The truth, it seems, is more apt in Michael's novel to appear in "things that could only be guessed at" than in hard facts, which are always, or usually, more complicated than we wish to believe.

To think of *Anil's Ghost* in this way is to see—or so I believe—that it is at once a metaphysical thriller and a kind of political novel in which actions that can be confidently called by their rightful names—abduction, mutilation, deception, terror —vie for our attention with more mysterious factors, like love, bereavement, betrayal. One reviewer of the novel noted that Michael's books move "across a shocking gap of weightlessness," but weightless is precisely what these novels are not. Though they are hedged, everywhere, by mystery, and, quite as the reviewer says, "backlit in legend," the characters and their actions are always also earthbound. Even where characters hover somewhere above familiar ground, searching not always resolutely for facts and footholds and leads and contexts, they never lose entire contact with the intimate, the familiar, the recognizable. Often they are drawn, like their author, to the unknowable, or at least the unknown, because they mistrust what is too easily understood, too readily susceptible to empathy or blame or summation. Mystery in *Anil's Ghost*, as in Michael's other fiction, is most often a way of signaling the mind's resistance to the obvious and the falsely comforting.

In effect, this resistance is a form of moral reflection. It is Michael's way of recording and responding without making flat-footed speeches or currying favor with readers by making appealing, politically correct noises. In *Anil's Ghost* we hear of terrible things. People confide to one another information we would rather not be privy to, shocking statistics, grotesque if abbreviated anecdotes, fragments of horror stories we know enough to believe in. But throughout this novel, which circulates so steadily in a realm rife with atrocity and impending disaster, where even intimate relationships are often painful and lovers and friends and brothers and husbands and wives are apt to do to one another what is not to be done, our sense is that there is always something that redeems, that lightens, that complicates. No part of the something else comes to us as distraction or escapist fantasy or mere wishful thinking. It emerges, always, from the very substance of the novel, and is an expression of what is deepest and truest in Michael's imagination.

When other writers try to say about Michael what impresses them more than they can say, they say he is a poet, by which they mean that he has a true instinct for the sublime, the preternatural, the just-beyond-the-range-of-ordinary-language, the quiet, that which politics can't finally touch or understand any more than most of us can touch it or understand it when we are in what we call our right mind. *Anil's Ghost* travels even further than Michael's previous books into the darkness he has taught us to expect and to trust him to navigate for us, and though it is a fearful journey he takes us on, we trust him still to make us grateful for the time we spend in that dark place, a place, as one of his characters is made to reflect, not solely "hard and feral" but, occasionally, "generous," susceptible to the "sweet touch" of a hand, the saving gesture of the artificer who knows the worst and wants if he can to make it better.

MICHAEL ONDAATJE [2001]

Great fiction seems usually to require a patient vigilance, a steady, growing searching out and gathering in that is central to the work of Michael Ondaatje. In fact, Michael's work never seems hasty, feverish, over-reaching. His is the work of a writer with no tendency to grab at easy resolutions or to editorialize or make speeches on current topics. Though there are, in his work, ideas, even, on occasion, issues, no reader will feel that Michael's words are written to promote anything at all. He is, in the best sense, a contemplative writer, with the rare and exquisite gift for probing the unspeakable and searching out dark places in the souls of his characters.

Of course words like patient and steady may fail to convey at all the feel of Michael's writing, the texture and organization of his books, which are distinguished by a formal restlessness. These novels of Michael's are, all of them, though in varying degrees, works perpetually in search of a form. Though they are never at loose ends, never recklessly assembled, they are intent on trying out seemingly incompatible narrative strategies, inviting vagrant motives, permitting characters now and then to drift off for a while, their relevance suspended. Often we have the sense that it is an oil sketch rather than an oil painting we are taking in, strokes deftly, lightly set down, the transitory and the gestural made to count for more than they would in any other set of authorial hands.

At least as telling is the language of Michael's fiction, the odd shifts in tense, the sudden dips, or lifts, into poetic diction, the sly obliquities of phrasing. In his recent novel, *Anil's Ghost*, the limpid even pristine declarative sentences may suddenly, briefly, give way to, "without her presence the gardener and sweeper and cook loosened away from necessity," a sentence that compels by virtue of its calculated oddness, its seeming almost to remind us of a sentence translated from some other language. Within a page or two of that sentence we come upon, " Gamini knew he had never been good company; small talk plunged to its death around him," a sentence at once metaphorically vivid and hauntingly connected—in a thoroughly unpredictable way —to the preoccupation with death and terror that permeates the entire novel. Just so, we are surprised by the almost casual poetry of many of Michael's sentences, their soft, almost inadvertent interruption of what had seemed brisk, workmanlike description. How often, in *Anil's Ghost*, does a blunt, simple sentence lead into a sentence like "the boundary between sleep and waking was a cotton thread so faintly coloured he often crossed it unawares." The image is, we note, precise and yet fragile in the way of the best poetic metaphors, the very quality of faint colouring attributed to the cotton thread just a bit risky, though in Michael's prose there is never a sense of straining for effect or of over-extending a silken metaphor.

We ought as well to note, as faithful readers of Michael's work, the delicate recourse to darkness and reverie. Often in *Anil's Ghost*, as in other books by Michael, we have the impression that we are caught up in a real-world narrative with an underlying ghost-story to which we have only faint, intermittent access. We do not want more of the ghost-story than Michael provides, or rather we know from the first that the shadowy outlines of the action that holds us are at least in part responsible for the deep interest we take in character and incident. We are gripped by dim aspects and uncertainties and only-partially-filled-in-mysteries that compel us because the novel obviously, genuinely wishes to understand them while hoping also to preserve that quality of the unknowable and the rare. When the poet Robert Duncan is suddenly quoted at the end of a fragmentary chapter of *Anil's Ghost,* to the effect that "the drama of our time. . . is the coming of all men into one fate," we do not take it that we must decide, then and there, whether or not the assertion is true, or whether it could conceivably be true. But we are moved by the ceaseless effort of Michael's writing to come to terms with everything, to engage the merely possible as if it were, truly, thinkable, to acknowledge what remains and is likely to remain obscure, while continuing to gesture at meaning and clarity as if they were as much a summons to him as the ineffable. This is, need I say, a great writer who seems always to write at the top of his form.

CYNTHIA OZICK [1990]

One of my favorite Cynthia Ozick fictions is a story called "The Suitcase." It appeared originally in a 1976 volume called *The Pagan Rabbi*, and it is striking not least for the fact that it seems a characteristic work while betraying none of the fondness for metaphysics and phantasmagoria so often associated with Cynthia's fiction. Here are no golems, no messiahs, no doubles or lost sons or half-crazed impostors. In certain wildly funny passages we might almost believe we had wandered into an arch comedy of manners, one part Henry James, another Oscar Wilde. Other passages bristling with charged references to the Nazi war against the Jews are yet without the darkness and solemnity seasoned readers of Cynthia's work might expect. Issues of guilt and historical responsibility are raised principally to provoke, amuse, bewilder, not to edify or explain. A brief exchange on the German manufacture of shampoo from Jewish body fat seems closer, somehow, to farce than to tragedy. Wit is exercised with an almost manic abandon, and without any indication that one target is much more important than another. To say that, in "The Suitcase," everything is grist for Cynthia's satiric mill is to accept that the imagination on display is darting, light and free, not at all the dutiful servant of an overmastering obsession.

Of course, the free play of imagination is very much in evidence in all of Cynthia's fiction, and she has often expressed her disdain for the trite and formulaic, the "arrested" and "parochial." Most often an ardent, even bruising writer, she has cultivated a fierce interest in matters bearing on Jewish fate and identity and, in so doing, invited the charge of the very parochialism she disdains. Though she has never published a trite or predictable sentence, she has seemed to some readers to write from a perspective so alien as to be almost inaccessible. We recall that Cynthia's stories often run to the fantastic and supernatural, that they betray a special feeling for paradoxes and riddles, and that often the primal force to which her characters respond most deeply is a Judaism remote or confounding even to those characters themselves. Adopting, in her fiction and in many of her essays, the language of ancient Jewish controversy, she writes of covenants and choral voices, of Diaspora and the redemptive. No wonder, to readers whose entire sense of presentness and relevance is shaped by post-modern discourse and minimalist fiction, Cynthia should seem a throwback to liturgical traditions and obsessions no longer widely compelling.

Needless to say, Cynthia has meanwhile attracted legions of devoted readers, for many of whom the idea that a visionary writer should be considered "parochial" is itself ridiculous. And of course, true readers know that Cynthia belongs in the company not of her co-religionists but of the writers who have changed the way we think and feel; not merely with important Yiddish writers and thinkers, but in the company also of other great writers, from Henry James and T.S. Eliot to Saul Bellow and Franz Kafka. Clearly, the stubborn minority resistance to Cynthia's work is generally symptomatic of a large failure of understanding. For Cynthia has, in one work after another, used myth and history and Judaic sources to raise questions of the greatest present urgency. What, she asks, is the relation between a dead language like Yiddish and the ostensibly living language of the modern and post-modern writers who confidently address a mass audience? What is lost and what is gained when we presume to speak to and for everyone? How deeply is meaning felt by those who live their entire lives in a present world untouched by any thought of the eternal? What are ideas to people who trade promiscuously in opinions and pride themselves on being open to newness? Such questions are raised with a combination of urgency and irony, with an intellectual rigor that places Cynthia at the furthest possible remove from sentimentality or parochialism. True, she yearns for some cultural or linguistic equivalent of the shtetl, for a new Jewish community whose writers will once again exercise their visionary imagination on questions of redemption and Law. But she knows—as only a great imaginative writer can know, to the root of her being—that what she desires is ever elusive, ever just beyond the capacity of language or intellect to embody it.

Cynthia knows, too, that the business of the Jewish writer has much in common with the work of other writers, who exult in telling stories and delight in their power to create. A Jewish writer like Cynthia may feel more than others the conflict between the desire to transmit sacred truths and the desire to freely exercise her imagination. But Cynthia is preternaturally alert to both desires, and the reader who supposes that she writes fiction simply to promote a particular religious imperative just doesn't know how to read very well. In no other contemporary writer is the tension between creative freedom and strictness of conscience so powerfully enacted and sustained. However much Cynthia may wish to cast her narratives as parables of law, obedience and conscience, her love of the ordinary, her feeling for literary realism, her suspicion of utopian political schemes, and her wildly irreverent instinct for satire and verbal play prevent her from making any ideological investment in her more extravagant projections.

It is tempting, in thinking of a writer who has given us many books—novels, stories, essays—to recommend these rather than those, to describe the arc of a progress or development.

But in the case of Cynthia Ozick this seems superfluous. From the periodical publication of her great stories "The Pagan Rabbi" and "Envy, or Yiddish in America" in the late 1960's, she has gone on to create a succession of palpable masterworks—inimitable, virtuosic, and full of every kind of moral intensity. In all of her writing an artist of lavish invention and iron command, she is also a writer of great comic range, capable of moving briskly from intellectual slapstick to literary parody, from cruel irony to audacious sleight of hand. The writer who early gave us vivid portraits of insanely jealous obsessives, charlatans and romantics went on in later years to invent a Sigmund Freud who dreams of becoming a God, a Lars Andemening who believes he is the son of the Polish writer Bruno Schulz, and a Puttermesser who, with the help of an enormous golem, tries to turn New York City into an earthly paradise.

There is no use in describing this memorable procession as a progress. For many years now Cynthia Ozick has given us a god's plenty of character and metaphor and dreaming. Her work is at once various and all of a piece, unpredictable and coherent. Edmund White was helpful when he wrote of Cynthia some years ago that "Judaism has given her what Catholicism gave Flannery O' Connor—authority, penetration, indignation." But we may be forgiven, I hope, if we amend this a little to say that Cynthia has made of her Judaism, as of her aesthetic predilections and moral convictions, an art that no dispensation—sovereign or otherwise—can confer. To read her is to know that what is quaintly referred to as the death of the author is a phenomenon greatly exaggerated and greatly misconceived. Cynthia Ozick is, in every sense of the term, a creator, the living author of works that terrify, delight, move and astonish.

DARRYL PINCKNEY [2001]

Darryl Pinkney's recent articles, published in *The New Yorker* and in *The New York Review of Books*, continue, no doubt, to secure his reputation as one of the most seductive writers on black America—on the manners and morals and disaffections of black and white America, to be more accurate. I say seductive in spite of the fact that Darryl is by no means a polemical writer, speaks for no particular constituency, offers to no set of readers anything like a satisfyingly predictable ideological agenda. With his combination of whimsy, eloquence, mournful nostalgia, self-disparagement and razor-sharp irony he creates a tone, and a persona, that are peculiarly astringent and affecting, at once charming and ever so slightly chilly. Here, we feel, is a witness, at once reporter and participant-observer, who seduces much of the time with wit, whose ambitions are always literary, whose observations never thicken into complacency.

For many of us, Darryl's articles, for all their brilliance and their importance in establishing a plausible, informed account of the works and days of leading black writers and intellectuals, will always seem secondary to Darryl's great first book, his novel *High Cotton*, published in 1992. To read this novel slowly, as it deserves to be read, is to feel on every page the sheer pleasure its author takes in language itself, in the creation of beautiful sentences, in surprising turns of phrase and reversals of expectation. There is nothing merely fine or flamboyant in Darryl's narrative prose, no gauzy language or over-clever metaphorical heavy lifting. The prodigious verbal gifts are harnessed to a variety of ends, and even where the metaphors are thick on the ground, we marvel at how much Darryl's characters mean to us, how invested we are in the meaning they have for Darryl, or his narrator, whose vision of things develops, however discontinuously, with enormous cogency and vitality.

Of course it is Darryl's experience that counts most for us in *High Cotton*, which reads like a novel deliberately cast in the form of a memoir. From the very first sentence, where the narrator declares no-one sat him down and told him he was a Negro, we are taken by his attempts to discover and evade his fate, to learn his identity and to avow that if he prefers, he can say it's no concern of his. Everywhere in Darryl's book the prose is nimble, the dominant aspect at once rueful and wry. A local, small-scale civil rights march featured, Darryl writes, "Leaders… driven by the code that said, 'I've written this out and you're going to hear every word.'" When the mini-protest breaks up, "people left abruptly," Darryl writes, "rolled away like beads of mercury." And where did this lead Darryl, or his narrator? "I wanted to hurry home," he says, " to sink back into that state where good news for modern Negroes couldn't find me." Delicious, that "good news for modern Negroes," the flip, dismissive, can't-be-bothered-with-this-nonsense tone not altogether obscuring the growing unease occasioned by the developing protest movement.

In fact we are absorbed, all through *High Cotton*, by Darryl's negotiations with his skeptical temper, his efforts at detachment and commitment, his desire to hold his "vaselined head" high and to believe it doesn't matter how he holds his head. At once an elegy for a certain kind of educated, "decent" Negro and a repudiation of that very type, *High Cotton* alternates between respect and cool disdain, between studied disaffection and a comedy of manners aspect that occasionally approaches parody and burlesque. In the end, Darryl's novel is a brilliant, patchy, erratic record of a persistent preoccupation with blackness, though we entirely believe him when he says, in ever so many ways, that he's tried all his life not to regard that preoccupation as the one single, central issue he was put on earth to engage. In the end, of course, as *High Cotton* and all of Darryl's other writing make clear, the man just can't help himself where this preoccupation is concerned. He is claimed by something inescapable, and he takes it on with a wit and mordancy unrivalled in recent American writing.

FRANCINE PROSE

The writer Jean Strouse once wrote that Francine Prose "documents the madness and grace of God in everyday life." It is an interesting if not perfectly accurate representation. There is something a little bloodless in the word *documents* which doesn't at all fit the tone of Francine's work, which is eccentric, sometimes whimsical, and even makes room for the fantastic. Nor does the reference to "everyday life" entirely capture what Francine's fiction is about. To be sure, Francine is interested in people, and she situates her characters in circumstances that are familiar, even humdrum. But Francine's most memorable fictions are tempted toward a vision of things that is anything but "everyday," and even her most satiric send-ups of spiritualist inebriates and new-age gurus betray an umistakable attraction to the weird and the miraculous.

The author of ten novels, several volumes of stories, and many miscellaneous works of non-fiction, Francine is of course one of the best known comic writers in the country. Often, her targets have been drawn from the comfortable American middle class, but her satire is readily directed at a wide range of types and conventions. Alert to the lunacies associated with the revolution in gender relations effected over the last two decades, she is equally interested in transformations in the family, childhood, and popular culture. Rightly said to have a "ventriloquist's skill in capturing contemporary jargon," she reminds us of how thoroughly our words and our thoughts and our intimacies have been shaped by the various culture industries. But in so reminding us, she never—never once—sounds like T.W. Adorno or any of the other German thinkers who have made some of us terminally self-conscious about the things we say. In fact, Francine writes sentences as admirable for their efficiency as for their wit, and her satire is as alert to possibilities of grieving and doubt as to openings for comic repartee.

Francine's latest novel, entitled *Hunters and Gatherers*, was published late last fall, and it is at once a characteristic work and a fresh encounter with new-age figures we recognize from her earlier novels. The literal-minded women of the new novel are every bit as given to unwitting self-parody as some of Francine's earlier protagonists. They are also vulnerable and picturesque, drawn to charismatic goddess-worshipping charlatans and shadowed by all-too-human conditions—physical illness, low self-esteem, disappointment in love, and so on. Which is to say that, like Francine's best fictions, her latest novel is never escapist, never *merely* funny or smart. Francine's is a comedy of insight and correction, recalling us to sanity even as it immerses us in the ludicrous and the inane. Yes, she *does* sometimes leave us laughing too hard for comfort. But hey, as one of Francine's people might say, or "yo," if it's easy comfort you want, this fiction isn't for you.

MARILYNNE ROBINSON [1994]

Marilynne Robinson is of course the author of two books. One, the 1981 novel called *Housekeeping*, is already a "classic" American novel. The other, *Mother Country*, published in 1989, is a brave and chilling environmentalist polemic that has aroused considerable surprise, legal action, and controversy. Marilynne has also written many essays, which she will one day collect for book publication, and she is working on a new novel which her many readers and friends are eager to see and to hold, completed, in their greedy hands.

Marilynne's stature as a leading American writer of course has everything to do with *Housekeeping*, a work that seems never to dim, not with re-reading, not with recapitulation. Many have said of it that it is a triumph of style, and of course it is, though that doesn't begin to get at its virtues. For what do we mean when we say that a work of fiction is a triumph of style? Not, surely, that it goes about its business with a resolute determination to evoke and to feel and to shape with no recourse whatever to a showy or artificial stylishness. And yet that is precisely the determination that is everywhere apparent in *Housekeeping*. On no page is there a sign of literary acrobatics or gaudy word-painting. The prose manages to be enthralling without any taint of over-reaching. Style is here precision, adequacy of means to purposes, control of voice, steady grasp of what needs to be said and what needs to be left alone.

In much the same way Marilynne sustains a wide range of atmospheric effects without the sort of patent heavy breathing or hold-your-breath dynamics all too familiar in other novels of mood. Melancholy in *Housekeeping* is conveyed as a pervasive ether to which human beings may grow so accustomed that they do not know what it is they feel. Loss and the fear of loss are elemental emotions characters move within, emotions palpable to them and to us even when they are so diffuse as to seem perfectly unnameable. Dream and illusion and drift are all of them a part of what Marilynne's characters experience, but these vague states are so sharply registered in the prose as to seem not merely "atmospheric" but essential aspects of character and psychology and theme.

I must mention too the novel's brilliantly eccentric handling of action. Very little happens in *Housekeeping*. There are no violent episodes or resonant reversals of fortune. Much of the narrative is designed to immerse us in routine, however much we sense the encroachment of disillusion and disorder. The miraculous achievement of the narrative is that it should generate such a deep, even elemental attachment to order and routine while steadily subverting that attachment, insidiously exposing its illusory character. We feel, emerging from *Housekeeping*, that we have understood, as if for the first time, the true horror of impermanence. But we feel, too, as we do when we read Keats, perhaps, that there is in the metaphysical design of the work before us some promise, some recompense, some sure manifest of the idea that, where there is loss, there may well be pleasure. *Housekeeping* is a novel that affords tremendous pleasure, a pleasure I can best describe by saying, simply and at last, that it places us firmly in a real world which is everywhere mysterious, more than a little terrifying, and never less than radiant with the promise of further revelation.

LYNNE SHARON SCHWARTZ [1996]

What makes a writer a model for other writers of more or less similar ambition? Call it touch, an impeccable ear, a confidence that has sometimes to do with wit, sometimes to do with just the right balance between immersion and detachment. In her short novel, *Leaving Brooklyn*, Lynne gives us the following very brief passage, told from the point of view of fifteen-year-old Audrey walking in on her parents' weekly card game: "The card game men were Mr. Zelevansky, Mr. Tessler, Mr. Ribowitz, Mr. Singer, and Mr. Capaleggio, who everyone called Cappy. Only I was expected to call them all Mr., and when for the first time—I was almost sixteen—I addressed Mr. Zelevansky, whom I had known all my life, as Lou, I felt as daring as if I had reached over and unzipped his fly."

We note in this what is obvious: the fluency in setting the scene, the establishment of the child's, or adolescent's, settled perspective, and the thoroughly surprising turn, which tells us a great deal about the—shall we call it seasoned?—intelligence that will filter the experiences offered to us in this book. The passage leaves us with a smile on our faces, and with the sure impression that the novelist has much to offer us in the way of pleasure and understanding.

The pleasures, in all of Lynne's fiction, come in various shapes, sizes, and degrees of duration. In a great tragic novel like *Disturbances in the Field*, one of my favorite contemporary American novels, there is the pleasure we associate with the steady immersion in lives worth knowing, in ideas worth grappling with. But there is, as well, an extraordinary range of smaller pleasures, sudden sharp impressions, stabs of color in the prose, odd codas appended to sentences. "Esther's voice," we read, "was deeper and coarser, with an alluring crack in it, like some magisterial old woman who has smoked all her life." Is it any wonder that Esther stands sharply in the mind, differentiated and herself quite in the way all of the other characters sharply emerge?

A student of mine, in a class for which I'd assigned a number of stories by Lynne, not long ago proposed that she might be a very intimidating model for an aspiring younger writer. She writes, my student said, as if every sentence really counts. Now I don't know that this is or has ever been intimidating to aspiring writers, but my student did surely put his finger on something that we like to think is true of all of our best writers. They make every sentence count—or at least we hope they do. With Lynne this observation is obviously borne out by just about everything she has given us. On page after page we find architecturally sumptuous paragraphs and great sentences. A woman with nightmares wakes up next to her man: "He is a very large, smooth man and she clings to him like a rock climber," Lynne writes. Elsewhere, in another work, a character thinks about friendship: "And then," Lynne writes, "years later, they tell us that there has never been any such thing as friendship among women, only rivalry, and that it is time to attempt Sisterhood. Sisterhood. The word has a grating sound. A friend is another self."

Of course it is easy to find even more richly textured sentences than these, where the language is tooled and inflected in ways that call to mind a more deliberately literary prose. But the point is that Lynne writes beautifully, with perfect tact and precision and timing at every turn, not merely at those moments when she is reaching for rare effects. And of course the more important point by far is that this writing is always in the service of the larger task of understanding the way we live, making sense of calamity and loss and probing the roots of our often inexplicable fellow-feelings. It is no wonder, none at all, that many of our best writers and readers, from Raymond Carver to Joyce Oates, from Anne Tyler to Sven Birkerts, have found in Lynne's writing a relentlessly absorbing density, beauty, and yes, an almost anthropological exactness in the recording of our characteristic modes of feeling and thought.

LYNNE SHARON SCHWARTZ [1997]

The narrator of Lynne Sharon Schwartz's recent novel, *The Fatigue Artist*, suffers from a malaise, an exhaustion, which preoccupies her throughout the various comings and goings of the book. But she confesses, not far from the end of the narrative, that her "ailment no longer interests me. It's tolerable only as I keep finding metaphors and stories to wrap it in." This is not at all a surprising revelation. Like her character, Lynne is and has long been a compulsive story teller and metaphor-maker. She has written a brilliant non-fiction book about reading-as-addiction, and her characters often are besotted with books and ideas. *The Fatigue Artist* is, among other things, a repository of reflections on stories and story telling. What is the relationship between the imaginary and the actual, she asks, often in the most explicit terms. "Fragments of ambivalence," her character Lama reflects, "beads on a string. The hard question in telling any story is, which are the beads and which is the string?"

The modernist self-consciousness about story telling which informs Lynne's latest novel directs us to a pervasive feature of her work. Though she is aptly describable as a realist writer, and has not repudiated realism in the way many of her contemporaries have done, she is a one of a kind species of realist. Her sentences sometimes observe themselves and reflect on the peculiar burden of their content. There is, in much of the writing, an eloquence that moves beyond the standard parameters of realist fiction. Even the language of physical description in Lynne's prose is a literary language, not willed, but inflected in the ways of the art novel. "She was a short, sturdy, honey-skinned Mexican woman," Lynne writes, "neither young nor old, wearing a plain black dress and white apron, not beautiful but emitting a benign glow, an allusion to the idea of beauty." Not at all the familiar language of the homely school of realist fiction, you'll agree, that "allusion to the idea of beauty."

Lynne has written several compelling books, and though it would be misleading to characterize her as a novelist of marital conflict, that has often been her subject. Both Rosellen Brown and Joyce Carol Oates praised her novel, *Rough Strife*, in those terms, and both Raymond Carver and Anne Tyler have concurred in their respective reviews of Lynne's fiction. All have seen in her work living persons and fully credible events. All have admired her careful documentation of settings and situations, her sensual evocation of character and relationship. Her novels, it is often said, "have an old-fashioned density," however much their attitudes or literary postures are in the service of contemporary ideas about the self.

But I resist the expression old-fashioned even as a partial characterization of Lynne's fiction. The sensibility in the fiction is too edgy and ironic to feel old-fashioned. The reflexiveness, even when it is not on full display, is always apparent, and whenever Lynne reflects on the novelistic itself in her fiction there is more than a hint of subversion in the air. Well along in her great novel, *Disturbances in the Field*, a character very pointedly contrasts fiction and reality. She plays with the classical notions of unity and proportion, and she describes "real time" as "dull and even, like a fox trot." Those of us who are taken in by the standard illusions promoted by most novels are gently satirized as irredeemably "middle-class," as readers who can somehow believe "that life should, [and will], reward good behavior." These observations, whether coming from Lynne or from one of her characters, are not the subversions of an old-fashioned writer promoting cozy pastimes inside securely ordered fictional worlds.

Lynne's novels—my favorites are *Leaving Brooklyn* and *Disturbances in the Field*—have been finalists for the Pen/Faulkner Award, and her stories have been included in *The Best American Stories*, The O'Henry Prize volume and many other anthologies. But I'll conclude by saying what seems to me just as important: every year, when I teach one of her novels in my fiction classes, I find that she speaks as powerfully to my students as she does to me and to other writers we admire.

JOANNA SCOTT [1998]

The recent June issue of *Harpers* magazine features a fierce, funny polemic by Francine Prose—due here late next week—which considers the question, "are women writers really inferior?" Of course many of us will wish to dismiss such a question—I have only to think Nadine Gordimer or Cynthia Ozick or Jamaica Kincaid to regard it as a somewhat preposterous question—but it is at the least interesting to note that a variety of unwarranted assumptions continue to control the thinking of some very sophisticated people, and that even some very good writers —men and women—still blithely assert that real men typically write "raw and undefended" prose beyond the reach of women, and that even the best women writers often betray "a certain narrowness" and a "predictability of technique."

I bring this up, here, because Joanna Scott told me about Francine's essay in conversation this week, and because her own work consistently refutes and confounds the hare-brained assumptions lightly anatomized in Francine's piece. For Joanna Scott is nobody's standard, narrow woman writer. She is nobody's quaintsy artsy needle-pointer, and her work is not limited to the brief run "between the boudoir and the altar." Neither is her prose neat or too sparklingly bright or in any way stillborn. Her fictions are neither cautious nor diminutive. In fact, to think of Joanna Scott is to think of a writer charged with large energies and large ambitions and equipped with a repertoire of devices expansive enough to achieve the most far-ranging purposes.

Joanna's first novel, *Fading, My Parmacheene Belle*, recently re-issued in a paper edition, was commended for its audacious invention and its metaphorical brio. Anything but safe and tidy, it offended some timid reviewers put off by its relentless eloquence and by its unembarrassed commitment to fabulation. A domestic fiction? Not by a long shot. A novel of cozy interiors and nice sentiments? Not at all.

No more would anyone think to pigeonhole as merely woman's fiction Joanna's brilliant 1991 novel, *Arrogance*, built around the life of the Austrian painter, Egon Schiele. For *Arrogance* is a harsh and uncompromising work, with a demanding collage-like structure, a freight of discursive elements, and characters who can seem brutish and appalling. Filled, as one very astute reader had it, "with a fin de siecle aroma of elegant and sensual corruption," the novel is distinguished by its masterful handling of setting and circumstance and by its resistance to the simple appeal of safe, linear narrative. I know of few recent novels more bracing and robustly appealing.

But then Joanna is always a bracing and surprising writer, interested in charting the treacherous borderline that separates reality from illusion, offering, much of the time, teasingly contradictory versions of the motives that drive her characters, probing obscure corners of history, elaborating richly textured motifs that fill us with a sense of the marvelous. Her collection of stories, entitled *Various Antidotes*, features a seventeenth century lens grinder, a Swiss scientist who studies the life cycle of bees, and a man named William Burke who was hanged in 1829 for murdering people and selling their cadavers for medical use. Her recent novel, *The Manikin*, is a kind of exuberant gothic novel, continuously eventful and full of wonders. One recent critic—a male critic, by god—asks whether it might not be fair to call Joanna—I shudder even to breathe the epithet—a domestic writer, but then he quite rightly intones, "but what dark domesticity, in which the kitchen is less inviting than the laboratory. Is Scott then our modern Mary Shelley?"

Well, no, I say—Mary Shelley could never have written *Arrogance*, never have managed its spare, disjunctive menace, and in any case, Joanna is interested in a lot more than laboratories, in a lot more than polishing the glass eyeballs in the cabinet of curiosities. And those of us who have seen what she can do as a novelist, who love and admire what we've seen, know we've but barely begun to imagine what lies just ahead for such a writer.

JULIA SLAVIN [2001]

The opening story in Julia Slavin's book, *The Woman who Cut off her Leg at the Maidstone Club*, is so funny and sustained and virtuosic that no reader will fail to be surprised that other stories in her book are equally good. Julia writes stories whose premises are so provocative and full of implication that you might almost suppose she needed, as a writer, to do little more than stick to the premise, never to betray it or abandon it. And in fact there is much to be said for that writerly program with a writer who is cunning and inventive, adept at creating a large metaphor to dominate and inform the development of her witty narratives. In that opening story, for example, entitled "Swallowed Whole," a young suburbanite swallows the adolescent yard worker she has been lusting after. The premise calls to mind the obvious antecedent fictions, from Kafka's *Metamorphosis* to the stories of Tomasso Landolfi in books like *Gogol's Wife*, and to be sure there is a certain pleasure in thereby placing Julia's fiction, settling it perhaps too neatly into a particular great tradition. But of course placement is no substitute for the attempt to see what is most distinctive in a new voice, what makes Julia's work not only accomplished by the standards of an identifiable genre or sub-species but truly original, with an accent all its own.

Julia's story, in fact, while it does belong in a tradition that includes Kafka and Landolfi, to say nothing of an American fabulist like Steven Millhauser, also calls to mind altogether different writers, not-always-stoic comedians of suburban American life, like John Cheever and John Updike, though the tone and texture of Julia's writing do not at all resemble theirs. Julia's fiction, in other words, has its own peculiar work to do, its own various, unpredictable, eclectic resources, and no reading of her stories governed by expectations strictly associated with the work of predecessor figures can account for the lavish pleasures to be found in her book.

This is not the place, obviously, for the close reading or detailed appreciation Julia's stories deserve, but I will say that each of the epithets that come most readily to this one reader's mind is both suggestive and unduly limiting. Take, as an example, the word grotesque. Yes, Julia's stories display a characteristic tendency to the grotesque, including a fondness for varieties of delicious excruciation and—to cite one concrete example—for a connoisseur's close examination of a puddle of vomit. There is no trace in this of the sophomore's guilty pleasure, no sense that, in indulging an appetite for the grotesque, the writer is exercising some forbidden pleasure, violating some oppressive decorum. The grotesque is in these works a fully established manner, a way of doing the necessary business of this writer's imagination, and it needs no justification beyond the author's obvious mastery of her chosen modality.

But if the word *grotesque* suggests heartlessness, or writerly self-indulgence, or a preference for atmosphere and obsession over everything else, well, then the word will only partially point to the heart of Julia's stories. They are, after all, in their way, rueful social criticism, ambivalent, bemused chamber pieces in which the milder pleasures of smooth green lawns and child-rearing and placid blue skies are intermittently glimpsed and entertained, stories with an unmistakable capacity for affection which is never bitter, never dismissed with the satirist's typically disillusioned skepticism. The floor beneath the feet of Julia's characters may be subject to strange eruptions and dislocations; her characters are, to be sure, given to self-destructive urges and paroxysms of waywardness; the settled life in the stories is never settled for good and all, and shouldn't be. The mild and the ordinary are, of course, sitting ducks for subversion and satire. But it is, somehow, a genial species of subversion Julia practices, her comic wit an instrument capable of playing in several registers which include the hilarious and the somber, the beautiful and the obscene.

Like Rick Moody, I believe that Julia has written one of "the most singular and arresting" books of short fiction of the last decade, and it is my pleasure to introduce her.

SUSAN SONTAG [1999]

It's tempting to think about Susan Sontag in the terms she proposed many years ago in a remarkable essay on Albert Camus. " Great writers are either husbands or lovers," the essay begins. "Some writers supply the solid virtues of a husband: reliability, intelligibility, generosity, decency. There are other writers in whom one prizes the gifts of a lover, gifts of temperament rather than of moral goodness. Notoriously, women tolerate qualities in a lover… that they would never countenance in a husband, in return for excitement, an infusion of intense feeling. In the same way, readers put up with unintelligibility, obsessiveness, painful truths, lies, bad grammar—if, in compensation, the writer allows them to savor raw emotions and dangerous sensations. And, as in life, so in art, both are necessary, husbands and lovers. It's a great pity when one is forced to choose between them."

This opening has always seemed to me, for as long as I can remember, a thrilling and audacious introduction, not only to Camus, but to thinking about writing generally. It opens up essential distinctions and suggests, in a way that is at once emphatic and playful, that one need not be imprisoned in a narrow preference, however much a given sensibility may incline us towards this sort of thing rather than that, to the irreverent or disorderly rather than the formally austere or fastidious, to the earnest or didactic rather than the decadent.

Of course Susan Sontag herself is a writer who has long defied categories. Deeply inquisitive about everything, she has often declared allegiance to a dizzying range of artworks and ideas. Justly celebrated for her fearless explorations of avant-garde film-making and photography, of camp and pornography, she has also taught us how to think about and make contact with the past. Deeply invested in the culture and politics of her own present moments, she has steadily enlarged our sense of all that is required to engage the present, most recently in Sarajevo and in Kosovo. A rationalist, a skeptic, a writer of impeccable lucidity, she has often directed our attention to the wayward and obsessive. Alert to the easy posturings and self-deceptions of writers committed to bland didacticism, she has nonetheless often written with enormous moral urgency and refused to settle for a fastidious aestheticism.

Susan has had several related and overlapping careers —as film-maker, cultural historian, essayist, playwright, short story writer and novelist. In her many previous visits to the Summer Writers Institute she has read from a play built around Alice James, from her novel *The Volcano Lover* and from several unforgettable stories including "The Way We Live Now." It is customary to think of work in different genres as coming from drastically different places in the head and heart, to think of essays, for example, in John Updike's terms as a species of hugging the shore. But Susan's essays have never felt in the least bit snug or secure and her fictions are typically as loaded with idea and aphorism, speculation and conundrum, as her essays.

Susan's 1992 novel, *The Volcano Lover*, sometimes reads like a biographical work, at other moments like a historical novel or an exquisitely deft philosophical discourse, though characters and situations are developed with the penetration appropriate to a work of fiction. Exotic particulars proliferate with a becoming thickness, and the air is sometimes dense with the cries of multitudes. Characters say amusing and witty things, and the novelist reflects in characteristically provocative ways about them. The past emerges as another country only fitfully related to our own but consummately interesting, a source of constant refreshment. Everywhere there are odd ideas, brilliantly pointed apercus, memorable phrases, characters we would like to have met, even in the less attractive phases of their lives. And we do get to know them in Susan's pages, do get to feel the steady pressure of their affections and antagonisms and enthusiasms. *The Volcano Lover* is a work of restless invention, at one moment invested in person and motive and betrayal, then gracefully moving off to wonderfully stylish interpolations. Caught up in the music of Susan's novel, we are not entirely certain what exactly we like best about it, so entirely are we given over to all of its charges and devices and grace notes.

And so, we say, the solid, husband-like virtues of Susan's novel are very much spoken for, amply represented, but we think of her—we must think of her—as offering principally to us the excitements and ravishments of a lover, so that in all of her work we find an infatuation with ideas, a fascination with form, an appetite for anachronism and for testing or surpassing boundaries, a voice alternately sensual and severe, agitated and Olympian. Those of us who have read one or two fragments of the new novel, entitled *In America*, that Susan will soon deliver to us, are eager to have it and to see what form exactly Susan's "spendthrift openness"—that's a phrase applied to Susan by Elizabeth Hardwick—will have assumed.

SUSAN SONTAG [2000]

"America is meant to mean everything," Maryna says in Susan Sontag's new novel, *In America*, and for much of the novel we are inclined to believe this great Polish actress, who comes here and achieves great success on the American stage. Just so do we believe her when she declares that it wasn't "a new life" she wanted but "a new self." Possibility and self-fashioning are everywhere on the horizon of Susan's large and generous book. And of course America is so entirely the right and inevitable occasion for the main action of Susan's novel because, in her hands at least, it is an instigation to freedom and imagination. The problem, as Susan's novel powerfully suggests, is that the American newness can sometimes feel, as she says, like "a new illness, the inability to become attached to anything."

Of course it is the faculty of will that has often seemed best suited to negotiating the odd tension between possibility and memory, between our sense of ourselves as limited beings with a past and that other sense of ourselves as potentially new, ever capable of pressing forward to some further transformation. And it is will that Susan invokes persistently in her novel. "I must and I will," declares her protagonist Maryna, who gives herself over to projects that may seem to others improbable, but to her compelling, as "ordeals, challenges, mystery" are compelling to one who needs to feel, as she says, "not at home." To Maryna, nineteenth century America is seductive because it seems "a whole country of people who believe in the will."

But will is only and ever will, as Susan's novel copiously and impressively demonstrates. Even great projects flourish only in time to deteriorate. Passions flare, and yield, or diminish, or confront disappointment. The commitment to the unconventional, to the ever fresh and contested can seem somehow conventional or safe when set beside more radical instances of newness. The really hot, or reckless, to which one gives oneself with all the force of one's will, may soon seem a mere transitory episode. The determination to live for art may begin to look like another way of living for oneself. The will is confronted, in Susan's novel, ever and again, by what cannot be willed, and the romance of idealism and renewal, of America as a vivifying state of mind, is made to assume the stature of a merely wonderful idea, or a great hope. When Susan's Maryna, late in the novel, reflects that perhaps "a happy life is impossible, and the highest a human being can attain is a heroic life," she is bearing witness to her own stubborn, brave imagination and to the limits of will.

Susan's novel is not by any means—in spite of what I have said here—a mere novel of ideas, any more than it is, what others have mistakenly supposed, a historical novel aiming to provide simply what such a work essentially offers. In fact, it is hopeless to assign to such a work an all-purpose epithet. Yes, *In America* has some of the period detail and charm of a brilliantly appurtenanced historical novel, and yes, it is consistently adventurous and adept in the mounting of ideas. But Susan gives herself to her characters in a way that makes them and their thoughts and abruptnesses and susceptibilities irresistible. The full-voiced, often operatic, intensity of the many-featured narrative in no way removes us from the characters. We are as much invested in them as any novelist could hope, and no aspect of the novelistic self-consciousness early on display in Susan's opening chapter is permitted to interfere with Susan's loving absorption in the fates of her characters. We revel in the novel's structural ploys and conceits, but never once do we feel that they are present to distract us from the primary business of the novel, which is embodiment and inquiry, the deliberately perilous management of emotion and the performance of what James Wood rightly calls "a certain buoyant irony, which breaks into true creative gaiety." Nowhere else in Susan's work, not in her great essays, not in her earlier novel *The Volcano Lover*, is that quality of creative gaiety so steadily palpable. Through all of its reflections on truth and lie, on the authentic and the mimetic, through all of its worldliness and its aesthetic infatuations, *In America* remains a book of great, contagious affection for life and for the making of art. It knows that the enemy of the good is the bland and that the pursuit of "the beautiful and true" will sometimes seem empty or specious. But Susan's book is ever in pursuit of the good and the true and the beautiful, and its love for its characters and their several ambitions is never bland. Though, in the great closing monologue of the novel, Susan's speaker, the actor Edwin Booth, declares that the artist is, must be, "turbulent, rarely affable", and must display the "vein of rage," Susan risks in her new book a turbulence that is loving, and affable, and mostly without the often disfiguring "vein of rage" that turns out to be, in this brilliant and various novel, largely, blessedly, but one possible dimension of the creative imagination.

ROBERT STONE [2000]

"There are two basic facts in life," Robert Stone has written. "We are out here in this stuff. And we are not alone out here. Fortunately, we have each other. Unfortunately, we have each other."

There is, in these few brief sentences, a good deal of Bob Stone, for starters, the strange combination of unillusioned realism and a certain stubborn hopefulness. And then you look at the word *stuff*, and you think, yes, that too is the right word for Bob Stone's kind of realism, where the novelist invests heavily in particulars and circumstances, in complicated ideas and intricate plot mechanisms, and yet invests with a sense that, however much you know, you are apt to feel you never really know enough. You are, Bob says, "out here in this stuff," and you may well believe you understand what's really going on as little as you did before you gathered the evidence and drew the conclusions.

This is not, in Bob's work, a descent into nihilism or a cynical repudiation of thought or learning, but it is part of a considered reflection on the often opaque nature of motive and experience. When Bob says, "From one moment to the next we hardly know what's going on, let alone what it all means," he says what his novels ceaselessly demonstrate. From Vietnam to Central America, from New Orleans to Jerusalem, Bob's locations are alike in one single respect, namely, that they can come to seem radically unstable, a maelstrom of facts and settings that point and point and yet often seem to signify less than we expect. We read Bob's novels as willing students of incomprehension, with a desire to be enlightened but with no conviction that such a wish can be long satisfied.

Of course Bob's work often revolves around persons and sects and movements for which certainty is not only desirable but essential. Characters in the novels are typically subject to elemental cravings. They mistrust the ordinary and yearn instead for something extreme, decisive. In Bob's most recent novel, *Damascus Gate*, the protagonist is a decent man appalled by the fanaticism of the religious lunatics drawn to "timeless creeds", "blood and soil" and absolutes. Everywhere he turns Bob's decent, thoughtful, inquisitive man is affronted by madmen and spies, mystics and ex-junkies, Cabbalists and deranged polymaths. We are reminded of an earlier work like *A Flag for Sunrise*, where Bob studied the relation of revolutionary politics to religious or messianic faith in Central America. In the newer novel, more insistently than ever before in Bob's work, we see roiling currents of obsession and antagonism. The very twilight teems "with riddles," and even momentary gusts of sweetness turn rapidly to something fatal or foul.

Bob's work has often been hailed as a sign that American realism remains vigorous and attractive, and that surely seems fair enough. But the very word 'realism' conveys only a part of what we want to note, in closing, about Bob's fiction. For his writing is not easy to pin down. In the novels we find, by turns, writing that is spare and efficient alternating with passages of genuine lyricism and impassioned utterance. Bob's novels are never less than absorbing, architecturally brilliant, the dialogue sometimes witty, always efficient, the description never too full, but the whole evincing what James Wood calls a "squeezed reticence" that never seems over-managed. Best of all, the precision of Bob's writing, his steady, thorough penetration of every sustainable aspect of his material, never interferes with his ability to convey the full force of his central insight, which is, in Bob's words, that "whirl is king," that though there is out there "the inexpressibly beauti-ful," "things happen ruthlessly, without mercy," and that "being decent"—just decent—"is really hard."

ROBERT STONE [2001]

I remember reading somewhere that Robert Stone reveres Samuel Beckett above all other writers, in part for his humor, in part for his grasp of "the primal situation" common to us all. Only for a moment did this pairing seem to me improbable. Beckett, after all, hardly seems fit company for an essentially realistic novelist with an appetite for sprawling, crowded canvases and an interest in worldly things, in politics and movements and particular places and highly individualized characters. But of course there is, also, in Bob Stone's fiction a fascination with the absolute, with degree zero and the search for truth. And there is, more often than not in Bob's work, an air of blight or disillusion. His idealists, questers, students of apocalypse or fanaticism, all of them tend to confront varieties of nullity or sheer incomprehensible human folly. As another writer has noted, in Bob's work the "finer passions disintegrate when there is nothing—no religious principles, no cultural or political forms, no varieties of personal connection—to which one can entrust them. Uncorroborated and unsupported, what's best in people turns vile." And, we may add, when there are in view religious principles, political forms, instruments of human connection, Bob's characters find ways to betray their advantages, to turn conviction to fanaticism, good intentions to inanity. Sam Beckett may not be, precisely, a presiding presence in the work of Bob Stone, but it's not hard to see that the preternatural darkness of Bob's vision may owe a good deal to that informing writer's pristine desolations.

Of course Bob's prose owes nothing at all to Beckett, whose manner is so relentless, pinched, unforgiving that it can almost—almost—seem an affectation. By contrast, Bob's writing, whatever its occasional reticences and what one writer has called its "intelligently starved" dialogue, is more generous, more expansive, more detailed. It is not much concerned with achieving the tension that comes from an extreme compression or concentration of verbal resources. Never is Bob's writing a flight from material contingency, and if there is in his work genuine anguish, it is never merely spiritual or essentially bodiless. Many of the terms that come most readily to the minds of Beckett's enthralled novel readers—solipsism, negation, repetition compulsion—are entirely irrelevant to a consideration of Bob's characteristic style and outlook.

The writer who said of Beckett's fiction that "nothing, nothing at all, exists outside the narrator's own skull" would never for a moment think to apply those words to Bob Stone, whose absorption in the diverse, substantial, messy stuff of reality is everywhere palpable. Bob's writing is never austere or torpid, and the voices in his novels, however diverse, are at most intermittently self-obsessed. Whatever the roiling interior consciousness of a Stone narrator, whatever the metaphysical urgencies that may sometimes grip him, his words never seem anything but deeply attuned to reality, to the out-there that may be terrifying or awful but is also inescapable and, much of the time, so inexhaustibly interesting that it is impossible for him to shut his eyes to it.

Others have noted, and no doubt will again, the extraordinary speed of Bob's narration, his ability to write with subtlety and wit while, at the same time, quickening the pulses of readers "whose powers of response have been accelerated"—not dulled— "by a lifetime of movie-going." No reader of his novels will fail also to note the confident architecture of his books, their ability to contain and yet press ahead with complex actions while simultaneously developing a core issue or concern near or at the center of our attention, however vivid the several distractions. This is a writer, we feel, who has taken on the largest questions with a determination and intensity that are entirely admirable. By turns passionate, curious, indignant, vulnerable, he has produced a body of work that is open to contradiction and to the higher moral sentiments that lesser writers fear.

TATYANA TOLSTAYA [1999]

It's tempting on an evening such as this to dispense with secondary description and superlatives, to introduce Tatyana Tolstaya simply by reading aloud from her fiction or her essays. That, we feel, would do her justice. That would place before an audience a resonance so full and lush, so spirited and bristling, if occasionally also dreamy, that it can be mistaken for no other. But of course Tatyana herself is here to set before us her inimitable prose, and it hardly seems fair somehow to associate one's own puny voice with the capacious instrument Tatyana has fashioned. That instrument, that voice, as has well been said, might well have been proscribed under an older Soviet dispensation, and no doubt it strikes even contemporary western readers as brimming with personality and prodigality far beyond ordinary measure. To hear that voice rolling through one's own interior spaces is to feel that the language of prose can accomplish whatever its maker proposes. Other writers have used words like *rampage, racing* and *windborne* to describe Tatyana's prose, with its headlong cadences, its sudden eruptions and subversive metaphors. To appropriate it, even for purposes of an entirely friendly, not to say loving, introduction, I should have to think of myself as deserving in a degree that as yet seems—shall we say—remote.

Some years ago, writing in *The New York Review of Books*, the eminent Russian scholar Henry Gifford referred to Tatyana as "today widely recognized as the brightest star of her generation," and that estimate has in no way diminished. No doubt, the estimate has in part to do with what Gifford calls "an exceptional virtuosity in language which, unlike Nabokov's, makes for itself no ostentatious claims." The virtuosity is as readily apparent in the English translations we have read as in the Russian originals most of us—myself very much included—cannot read. Often the virtuosity is a matter of pitch or tone, as when a monologue captures a character's movement from hate to longing, from sour self-conscious reflection to manic self-abasement. Sometimes it is evident in the swift movement of the narrative from the comic to the melancholic, from the all too believable to the magical or absurd.

Through all the shifts and turns, the language is terribly alive, sensually alert—to heat and smell and flavor and the texture of clothing, and to the prospect that a dark sky will clear, dreariness dissipate, a cold walk refresh. A character's unexpressed love is, in Tatyana, "a homely, barefoot orphan." A cup of tea "was no ordinary cup" but "a loving cup, adroitly disguised as a comradely one." A coverlet, thrown over a bed, is observed "rumpling in a slow glide, slack and indifferent," descending "unevenly, riding handfuls of stale household air." Everywhere our minds and our senses are quickened, Tatyana's language steadily "planting the cleared terrain," as she has written, "trimming away dry knots," "grafting flowering branches into place and gathering the fallen fruit." Everything is, at least intermittently, suffused by dream, perhaps the dream Tatyana attributes to one character, "of a genuine red rose, pure and deep like the sound of a cello," though there are also, in Tatyana's work, other kinds of dream, distressing, subversive, occasionally even dreams of oblivion or enfeeblement, dreams "tearing off into the dark."

Tatyana is of course widely read and celebrated beyond Russia and beyond this country. Her fiction has been translated into sixteen languages, her two books of stories as readily available at a bookstore in Paris as in Milan or Munich or Madrid. Joseph Brodsky, who visited us here a few years ago just before his death, described Tatyana as "the most original, tactile, luminous voice in Russian prose today," and noted how routinely she has inspired comparison with Gogol and Chekhov and Mikhail Bulgakov, Russian authors with—shall we say—a nice following among 20th century writers and readers. Like these writers at their best, Tatyana has managed to invest marginal lives with wonder and dignity, to discover possibilities of beauty in the hopeless, to tell what feels like the humble truth while practising a wide range of literary feats that delight and surprise.

Though Tatyana is chiefly admired for her fiction, she has also won a large reputation as an essayist. Her wildly funny pieces, on subjects ranging from cookbooks to the life and politics of Boris Yeltsin, appear frequently in the pages of *The New York Review of Books*, and have drawn laughs and admiration from readers as diverse as Saul Bellow and Seamus Heaney. The essays are marked by qualities of wit and verbal play familiar to readers of the stories, but they also attest to Tatyana's impressive command of Russian history, politics and folklore. The reviewer who wrote of Tatyana's stories as a "rampaging Russian garden in summer bloom" captured in those words the characteristic mood of Tatyana's writing, the essays as well as the fiction. There is no one quite like her, no one in whom the hectic, flooding rush of language can so steadily encompass the uncanny and the humble, the arabesques of daydream and the soft drone of the quotidian.

About the Author

Robert Boyers is Editor of the quarterly *Salmagundi*, Tisch Professor of Arts and Letters at Skidmore College, and Director of the New York State Summer Writers Institute. His books include *Atrocity and Amnesia: the Political Novel since 1950* (Oxford University Press), *After the Avant Garde: Essays in Art and Culture* (Penn State University Press), and three books devoted to leading critics of the modernist era: Lionel Trilling, F.R. Leavis, and R.P. Blackmur (all three with the University of Missouri Press). He writes regularly on contemporary literature for *The New Republic*, and his essays on politics and culture appear in such magazines as *The American Scholar, Daedalus, Dissent, Tri-Quarterly,* and *Partisan Review.* His recent short fiction has appeared in *Michigan Quarterly Review, Southwest Review, Shenandoah, Parnassus,* and other magazines.